The
SUNDAY
GOSPELS
for
ORDINARY
TIME

The
SUNDAY
GOSPELS
for
ORDINARY
TIME

All the Sunday Mass Gospel readings for years
A, B and C from the Revised New Jerusalem Bible

With commentary and guidance for Lectio Divina by
ADRIAN GRAFFY

DARTON·LONGMAN + TODD

This book is dedicated to
Dom Henry Wansbrough,
monk and biblical scholar

First published in Great Britain in 2021 by
Darton, Longman and Todd Ltd
1 Spencer Court
140–142 Wandsworth High Street
London SW18 4JJ

Print book ISBN: 978-0-232-53478-8
eBook ISBN: 978-0-232-53479-9

Cover and interior illustration image by Lyn May,
www.lynmay.co.uk

A catalogue record for this book is available from the British Library.

Designed and produced by Judy Linard
Printed and bound in Great Britain by Bell & Bain, Glasgow

CONTENTS

SUNDAYS IN ORDINARY TIME

SOLEMNITIES AND FEASTS OF THE LORD

INTRODUCTION

THE LECTIONARY PRODUCED IN the wake of the Second Vatican Council (1962–1965) has been with us now for over fifty years. It continues to offer a broad selection of readings from all parts of Scripture.

The gospels on Sunday are the most obvious proclamation of the good news of Jesus Christ. Those who carried through the Council's reforms had the brilliant idea of dedicating a year to each of the Synoptic Gospels, Matthew, Mark and Luke, assigned respectively to Years A, B, and C, and of giving John pride of place in the seasons of Lent and Easter. Each gospel is shown to make a unique contribution to the understanding of Christ, and we are able to recognise more keenly the particular accents and interests of the separate evangelists.

These two volumes on *the Sunday Gospels* provide text and commentary on all the gospel readings that occur on Sundays throughout the three-year cycle adopted for the Sunday lectionary. The first volume considers the 'strong' liturgical times: Advent, Christmas, Lent and Easter. The second volume covers all the remaining Sundays, known as 'Sundays in ordinary time' (*per annum*). Included in the second volume are the solemnities and feasts of the Lord which from time to time fall on Sundays, and displace the celebration of numbered Sundays.

It is probably useful to explain the basic 'shape' of the liturgical year. The 'strong' seasons, Advent, Christmas, Lent and Easter, are never displaced. Ordinary Sundays cover the remaining time. Since the date of Easter varies, the block of Sundays of Lent and Easter shifts too. This means that the number of ordinary Sundays between Christmas and Lent changes, as does that of Sundays between Pentecost (the last Sunday of Easter) and Advent.

Years A, B and C usually offer readings from Matthew, Mark and Luke respectively. There are some exceptions to this. For instance, on Sundays 17-21 of Year B (Mark), chapter 6 of the Gospel of John is proclaimed, with its extensive material on the Bread of Life.

How does one work out what year to follow? Each Year begins with Advent but is identified by the numbered year which begins after Christmas. One simply has to add up the four digits in the year, and if they amount to a multiple of three the year will be Year C. Year A is therefore a multiple of three plus one, and Year B a multiple of three plus two. Thus the year 2019 was Year C, because 2 + 0 + 1 + 9 amount to 12, a multiple of three. Once you have successfully completed the calculation the other Years, of course, follow.

The text of the gospel used here is from the *Revised New Jerusalem Bible*. The work of Dom Henry Wansbrough, this recently published Bible has a freshness and a clarity which is unsurpassed. The scholarship is up-to-date, while the text, clearly written for today's listeners, nevertheless preserves cherished biblical ways of expression, such as 'Blessed are the poor in spirit' and 'Amen, amen I say to you.'

Each gospel text is given in full, and there follows a concise commentary, opening up lines of reflection for individuals and groups, preachers and congregations. The references to all the readings of a given Sunday and to the responsorial psalm are always provided. Each section concludes with two questions and two proposals for prayer, so that the reading becomes both personal and prayerful.

I hope you will find these volumes provide a gentle and informed companion to the gospel readings offered in the Liturgy of the Word week by week and year by year.

THE REVD DR ADRIAN GRAFFY

SUNDAYS
IN
ORDINARY
TIME

YEAR A

Second Sunday in Ordinary Time
(Year A)

John 1:29–34

The next day, he saw Jesus coming towards him and said, 'Look, there is the lamb of God that takes away the sin of the world. This is he of whom I said, "After me comes one who has passed ahead of me because he was before me." I did not know him myself, yet I came baptising with water so that he might be revealed to Israel.' And John bore witness, 'I have seen the Spirit come down on him like a dove from heaven and it rested on him. I did not know him myself, but he who sent me to baptise with water said to me, "The man on whom you see the Spirit come down and rest is the one who baptises with the Holy Spirit." I have seen and borne witness that he is the Son of God.'

Other readings: Isaiah 49:3, 5–6   Psalm 39 (40)   1 Corinthians 1:1–3

DESPITE THE FACT THAT we have now re-entered the 'ordinary time' of the liturgical year, there is something of a reluctance to leave the Christmas season behind. The first reading, just like last Sunday, is taken from the 'songs of the servant' in the book of Isaiah. This time we hear that the servant is to bring light and salvation 'to the ends of the earth'. There is a clear echo here of the feast of the Epiphany and the people of the earth seeking the light of God. Furthermore, the gospel reading today is taken from the first chapter of John. We shall have to wait until next week to begin listening to the account of Jesus' ministry found in the Gospel of Matthew, the gospel laid down to be read this year.

The Gospel of John, known also as the 'Fourth Gospel', contains in its first chapter the magnificent 'prologue', read at Christmas, which begins with the mighty words 'In the beginning was the Word.' There follows a portrayal of John the Baptist, which differs in many ways from his presentation in other gospels. As shown in today's gospel, for this evangelist John the Baptist is above all a witness. There is no detailed presentation of the baptism of Christ. Rather, the Baptist proclaims the abiding presence of the Spirit with Jesus. This evangelist is not interested in the self-abasement of Jesus in accepting baptism from John, but focuses on the witness to Jesus given by the Baptist.

In this gospel reading John points out Jesus with the words: 'There is the Lamb of God!' These words recall the Passover lamb, slaughtered at the exodus from Egypt and year by year in the Jewish Passover feast. As the blood of the lamb was a sign of salvation for the Jews in Egypt, so the blood of Christ brings God's salvation and freedom to those who accept him.

Do I accept John's witness to Jesus?
How does the Fourth Evangelist present John the Baptist?
We pray with the Church: 'Lamb of God, you take away the sins of
   the world. Have mercy on us.'
We pray for a united witness from Christians to the truth which
   Christ brings.

Third Sunday in Ordinary Time (Year A)

Matthew 4:12–23

Hearing that John had been arrested he withdrew to Galilee, and leaving Nazara he went and settled in Capernaum, beside the lake, on the borders of Zebulun and Naphtali. This was to fulfil what was spoken by the prophet Isaiah:

> *Land of Zebulun! Land of Naphtali!*
> *Way of the sea beyond Jordan.*
> *Galilee of the nations!*
> *The people that sat in darkness*
> *have seen a great light;*
> *on those who lived in a country and shadow of death*
> *a light has dawned.*

From then onwards Jesus began his proclamation with the message, 'Repent, for the kingdom of Heaven is close at hand.'

As he was walking by the Lake of Galilee he saw two brothers, Simon, who is called Peter, and Andrew his brother; they were making a cast into the lake with their net, for they were fishermen. And he said to them, 'Come after me and I will make you fishers of people.' And at once they left their nets and followed him. Going on from there he saw another pair of brothers, James son of Zebedee and his brother John; they were in their boat with their father Zebedee, mending their nets, and he called them. And at once, leaving the boat and their father, they followed him.

He went round the whole of Galilee teaching in their synagogues, proclaiming the good news of the kingdom and curing all kinds of disease and illness among the people.

Other readings: Isaiah 8:23–9:3   Psalm 26 (27)   1 Corinthians 1:10–13, 17

TODAY WE BEGIN OUR reading of the story of the ministry of Jesus in the Gospel of Matthew, which will take us until the end of the liturgical year. We hear the evangelist's summary of Jesus' message: 'Repent, for the kingdom of heaven is close at hand.' Matthew precedes this with a quotation from the Hebrew Scriptures, which he declares to be fulfilled. Jesus brings light not only to Israel but to the nations too, to all those who 'live in darkness'.

From the very start he calls disciples. They leave everything at once to follow Jesus. The message of Jesus and his very personality invite them to take this risk. They accompanied him as he 'went round the whole of Galilee'. This is the first location for the preaching of the good news and for the healings of Jesus, the place where the gospel is warmly welcomed. We will hear more about these activities in the weeks to come.

Have I allowed Jesus to transform the darkness of my life?
Am I willing to leave everything and follow him?
We pray for a renewed openness to hearing the gospel on this Sunday of the Word of God.
We pray for all disciples of the Lord.

Fourth Sunday in Ordinary Time (Year A)

Matthew 5:1–12

Seeing the crowds, he went onto the mountain. And when he was seated his disciples came to him. Then he began to speak. This is what he taught them:

'Blessed are the poor in spirit, for the kingdom of Heaven
    is theirs.
Blessed are the gentle, for they shall inherit the earth.
Blessed are those who mourn, for they shall be comforted.
Blessed are those who hunger and thirst for righteousness,
    for they shall be filled.
Blessed are the merciful, for they shall receive mercy.
Blessed are the pure in heart, for they shall see God.
Blessed are the peacemakers, for they shall be called
    children of God.
Blessed are those who are persecuted in the cause of
    righteousness, for the kingdom of Heaven is theirs.

'Blessed are you when people abuse you and persecute you and speak all kinds of evil against you falsely on my account. Rejoice and be glad, for your reward will be great in heaven; this is how they persecuted the prophets before you.'

**Other readings: Zephaniah 2:3; 3:12–13   Psalm 145 (146)
1 Corinthians 1:26–31**

MATTHEW'S GOSPEL IS A gospel of teaching. It celebrates Jesus as the great teacher, who surpasses even Moses. The evangelist sets down five major speeches of Jesus in the course of the gospel, and the first of these is the famous Sermon on the Mount. Jesus, like Moses, goes up the mountain. He sits down and begins to speak.

The beatitudes, which open the Sermon, are a type of saying already found in the Old Testament and adopted by Jesus. The beatitudes of Jesus present a radical challenge to commonly accepted ideas. Jesus proclaims that the poor are 'blessed' or 'happy', not the rich. It is the gentle, the meek, who will inherit the earth, not those who are violent.

Eight beatitudes describe eight qualities or situations, such as those who mourn, those who show mercy, those who are persecuted. Each of these qualities or situations is described by Jesus as a special channel of God's favour. Jesus presents what we might call the 'scandal' of the gospel, a profound challenge which invites us to reconsider and to change the way we think and the way we behave.

The passage ends with a final beatitude, this time spoken directly to the disciples of Jesus: 'Blessed are you'. How can we possibly consider persecution and abuse to be blessings? If we can unite our own sufferings with those of Christ, we can begin to know God's presence in an entirely new way. With his very first words of teaching, Jesus calls us to radical change.

Is it absurd to look upon personal suffering as a gift from God?
What should our attitude be to the suffering of others?
We ask for the strength to transform our attitudes and behaviour.
We pray for all those who are persecuted and abused.

Fifth Sunday in Ordinary Time (Year A)

Matthew 5:13–16

Jesus said to his disciples, 'You are the salt of the earth. But if salt loses its taste, what can make it salty again? It is no longer good for anything, and can only be thrown out to be trampled underfoot. You are the light of the world. A city built on a hilltop cannot be hidden. No one lights a lamp and puts it under a tub; they put it on the lamp-stand where it shines for everyone in the house. In the same way your light must shine for people, so that they may see your good works and give praise to your Father in heaven.'

Other readings: Isaiah 58:7–10   Psalm 111 (112)   1 Corinthians 2:1–5

WE CONTINUE OUR READING of the great discourse of Jesus which we know as the Sermon on the Mount. Last week we read its famous opening verses, the Beatitudes. With statements such as 'Blessed are the poor in spirit, for theirs is the kingdom of heaven' Jesus challenges our attitudes and our actions.

This week, as Jesus continues addressing the disciples, he uses two simple images, salt and light. We are familiar with the phrase 'salt of the earth' when it is applied to people judged to be really good, even exceptional, but not everyone will know that these are originally the words of Jesus. On reflection we might consider it rather strange. Someone who 'rubs salt in a wound' adds insult to injury. Such is not Jesus' meaning here. Rather we need to think of how salt enhances the taste of a meal.

Jesus is actually talking about salt which has lost its taste and which is good for nothing but to be thrown away. The challenge he is putting before the disciples is the risk of losing their zeal, losing their enthusiasm for his message, and thereby offering people something weak and insipid instead, something short of the good news. If we begin to present only the easy parts of the good news, we risk offering something which does not deliver the fulness of life.

The second image is that of light, a much easier image to understand. These words of Jesus have given rise to the popular phrase 'Don't hide your light under a bushel!' People often speak of 'following their dreams', considering that the way to self-fulfilment is to achieve 'what I want' regardless of others. The life-giving challenge Jesus brings is that we should allow our light to shine, but that it is the light given us by Christ. The true greatness of the Christian is to offer to others Jesus and all the hope that he brings, by lives which are transparently good, full of salt and light.

Do we accept the fulness of the good news, or only the easy bits?
Do we allow our light to shine, or do we 'hide it under a bushel'?
We ask for the courage to live the gospel to the full.
We pray for strength to witness to the truth of the gospel for those we meet.

Sixth Sunday in Ordinary Time (Year A)

Matthew 5:17–37

Jesus said to his disciples, 'Do not think that I have come to abolish the Law or the Prophets. I have come not to abolish but to complete. Amen I say to you, till heaven and earth pass away, not one dot, not one little stroke, will pass from the Law until everything is achieved. Therefore, anyone who infringes even one of the least of these commandments and teaches others to do the same will be called least in the kingdom of Heaven; but anyone who keeps them and teaches them will be called great in the kingdom of Heaven.

'For I tell you, if your righteousness does not surpass that of the scribes and Pharisees, you will never get into the kingdom of Heaven.

'You have heard that it was said to our ancestors, "*You shall not murder*"; and whoever murders must answer for it before the court. But I say this to you, anyone who is angry with a brother or sister will answer for it before the court; anyone who calls a brother or sister "idiot" will answer for it before the assembly; and anyone who calls a brother or sister "fool" will answer for it in hell fire. So then, if you are offering your gift at the altar and there remember that your brother or sister has something against you, leave your gift there before the altar, go and first be reconciled with your brother or sister, and then come and offer your gift. Come to terms with your opponent in good time while you are still on the way to the court together, or your opponent may hand you over to the judge and the judge to the attendant, and you will be thrown into prison. Amen I say to you, you will not get out till you have paid the last coin.

'You have heard that it was said, "*You shall not commit adultery*." But I say this to you, anyone who looks at a woman lustfully has already committed adultery with her in his heart. If your right eye causes you to stumble, tear it out and throw it away; for it is better for you to lose one part of yourself than to have your whole body thrown into hell. And if your right hand causes you to stumble, cut it off and throw it away; for it is better for you to lose one part of yourself than to have your whole body go to hell.

'It has also been said, "*Anyone who divorces his wife must give her a writ of dismissal.*" But I say this to you, everyone who divorces his wife, except for the case of an illicit marriage, makes her commit adultery; and anyone who marries a divorced woman commits adultery.

'Again, you have heard how it was said to the ancients, "*You must not break your oath, but must fulfil your oaths to the Lord.*" But I say this to you, do not swear at all, either by heaven, since that is God's throne; or by earth, since that is his footstool; or by Jerusalem, since that is the city of the great King. Do not swear by your own head either, since you cannot turn a single hair white or black. Let your word be, "Yes, yes", "No, no"; anything more than this comes from the Evil One.'

Other readings: Ecclesiasticus 15:15–20   Psalm 118 (119)
1 Corinthians 2:6–10

WE CONTINUE READING FROM the first great speech of Jesus in the Gospel of Matthew, the Sermon on the Mount.

Jesus teaches that the 'Law and the Prophets', by which he means the scriptural tradition of Jewish faith, are to be cherished. Nevertheless, these traditions are to be 'completed' or 'fulfilled'. The fulfilment brought by Jesus can be new and unexpected.

Having challenged the inadequate 'justice' or 'righteousness' of the scribes and Pharisees, Jesus presents a new way. He gives six examples of how his teaching deepens the traditional teaching of the Jews. These pieces of teaching are sometimes described as 'antitheses'. In them Jesus quotes the Jewish tradition and goes on to challenge it with the words 'But I say this to you!'

The first challenge makes more radical the commandment 'You must not kill'. For those called by Christ there are deeper demands. To hurl anger and insults at another is not the behaviour of a Christian. In the following verses Jesus will offer radical new understandings of other tenets of the Law. To hate one's enemy may have been considered acceptable in the tradition, but Jesus says: 'But I say this to you: Love your enemies!'

Am I ready to learn new things from the teaching of Jesus?

Do I cherish the teaching of the Law and the Prophets which prepared the way for Christ?

We pray for readiness to learn from the Scriptures and from the teaching of the Church.

We pray for a new attitude to those who have offended us.

Seventh Sunday in Ordinary Time (Year A)

Matthew 5:38–48

Jesus said to his disciples, 'You have heard how it was said: "*Eye for eye and tooth for tooth*." But I say this to you: offer no resistance to the wicked. On the contrary, if anyone hits you on the right cheek, offer him the other as well; if someone wishes to go to law with you to get your tunic, let him have your cloak as well. And if anyone requires you to go one mile, go two miles with him. Give to anyone who asks you, and do not turn away from one who wants to borrow from you.

'You have heard how it was said, "*You shall love your neighbour* and hate your enemy". But I say this to you, love your enemies and pray for those who persecute you; so that you may be children of your Father in heaven, for he causes his sun to rise on the evil as well as the good, and sends down rain on the righteous and the wicked alike. For if you love those who love you, what reward do you have? Do not even the tax collectors do as much? And if you save your greetings for your brothers and sisters, are you doing anything exceptional? Do not even the gentiles do as much? You must therefore be perfect, as your heavenly Father is perfect.'

Other readings: Leviticus 19:1–2, 17–18   Psalm 102 (103) 1 Corinthians 3:16–23

IN THE SERMON ON the Mount, Jesus has stated his intention to bring the Law and the Prophets to fulfilment. Jesus challenges and deepens the Jewish law. He repeats: 'You have heard it said, but I say this to you!' In today's gospel we hear how Jesus presents two further tenets of the law.

The instruction 'eye for eye, tooth for tooth' was a way of ensuring that retribution, repaying evil for evil, did not get out of control. Punishment should always be proportionate to the crime committed. Jesus, however, instructs his disciples not to pay back evil for evil. This is a difficult teaching for people of today, and indeed of any time, for it urges us to endure without retaliating when evil is done to us.

The climax of this part of the Sermon on the Mount, the last of the series of 'antitheses' in which Jesus contrasts traditional teaching with his new way, involves the love of enemies. For traditional Jewish understanding hatred of enemies was allowed. But Jesus presents the love of enemies as basic to Christian life. Once again a stern challenge is thrown down to our natural inclinations and actions. It is not surprising that Jesus goes on to say: 'Be perfect as your heavenly Father is perfect!' To live the Christian life is to make God's compassion and love the measure of our actions. Jesus himself will live out these teachings. He will forgive those who crucify him.

Am I open to the challenges the gospel brings?
Do I take seriously the command to 'be perfect as your
heavenly Father is perfect'?
We pray for those whose lives are poisoned by hatred.
We pray for a new heart and a new spirit.

Eighth Sunday in Ordinary Time (Year A)

Matthew 6:24–34

Jesus said to his disciples, 'No one can be the slave of two masters: a person will either hate the first and love the second, or be attached to the first and despise the second. You cannot be the slave both of God and of money.

'Therefore I tell you not to worry about your life, what you should eat, nor about your body, what you should wear. Surely life is more than food, and the body more than clothing! Look at the birds in the sky. They do not sow or reap or gather into barns; yet your heavenly Father feeds them. Are you not worth much more than they are? Can any of you, by worrying, add one single cubit to your span of life? And why worry about clothing? Learn from the grasses of the fields, how they grow; they neither work nor spin, yet I assure you that not even Solomon in all his glory was clothed like one of these. Now if God so clothes the grasses of the field which are there today and thrown into the furnace tomorrow, will he not much more clothe you, who have so little faith? So do not worry; do not say, "What should we eat? What should we drink? What should we wear?" It is the gentiles who strive for all these things. Your heavenly Father knows you need them all. Strive first for his kingdom, and righteousness, and all these other things will be given you as well. So do not worry about tomorrow: tomorrow will take care of itself. Each day has enough trouble of its own.'

Other readings: Isaiah 49:14–15   Psalm 61 (62)   1 Corinthians 4:1–5

THERE ARE TWO THEMES in this excerpt from the Sermon on the Mount. In the first paragraph the question before us is: Are we to serve God or money, God or the things of this world?

The second paragraph brings in a related theme. If we choose to serve God, then we can rely on God's goodness to provide for our needs. Jesus' words have an extraordinary immediacy for the world of today. In so many ways we are enslaved to the values of the world. Our ideas and actions in relation to food have changed remarkably. More food is wasted than ever before by those who have it, and yet much of the world's population does not have the food it needs. Food has become a source of entertainment, rather than something which we need, something for which we thank God, and something we share.

It is similar with clothing. Many people have become obsessed not only by what they wear but also by their appearance. The quest to look perfect, often in a way which is counterfeit and sham, has entrapped many. Jesus says that these are the concerns of the 'pagans'. As Christians we must challenge the false values proclaimed around us, values which deceive and disappoint. We must set our hearts on God's kingdom and on God's righteousness.

Am I deceived by false and pagan values?
Am I obsessed with what I eat and how I appear?
Pray for detachment, that from our abundance we may provide for
    those in need.
Pray for a new spirit of gratitude and trust in God.

Ninth Sunday in Ordinary Time (Year A)

Matthew 7:21–27

Jesus said to his disciples, 'Not everyone who says to me, "Lord, Lord," will enter the kingdom of Heaven, only the person who does the will of my Father in heaven. On that day many will say to me, "Lord, Lord, did we not prophesy in your name, drive out demons in your name, do many deeds of power in your name?" Then I shall tell them to their faces: I have never known you; away from me, evil-doers! Therefore, everyone who hears these words of mine and acts on them will be like a sensible person who built a house on rock. Rain came down, floods rose, gales blew and hurled themselves against that house, and it did not fall: it was founded on rock. But everyone who hears these words of mine and does not act on them will be like a stupid person who built a house on sand. Rain came down, floods rose, gales blew and struck that house, and it fell; and what a fall it had!'

Other readings: Deuteronomy 11:18, 26–28, 32   Psalm 30 (31)
Romans 3:21–25, 28

OUR SUNDAY GOSPEL READING presents the final words of Jesus in the Sermon on the Mount, the first and most famous of the five long discourses of Jesus in the Gospel according to Matthew. The reading puts before us the challenge to take seriously the words of Jesus' preaching and to put them into practice.

Jesus speaks about 'doing the will of the Father'. There is an echo of the words of the Lord's Prayer. If we pray 'thy will be done', then we must play our part to make those words a reality. In the parable that follows, Jesus compares the actions of the wise man and the fool.

There are two ways of responding to Jesus' words. The lesson is clear.

As he concludes his account of the Sermon on the Mount, the evangelist Matthew is well aware that people often resist the words of Jesus. The first reading, from the book of Deuteronomy, asks us to allow the words of God's law to enter our hearts and our souls. There is a fundamental choice to be made between the way of life and the way of death. The challenge is 'set before us today'.

The second reading this Sunday is from St Paul's great but difficult masterpiece, the Letter to the Romans. 'God's justice', writes Paul, 'made known through the Law and the Prophets, has now been revealed'. Faith in Christ brings the promises made to the Jewish people to fulfilment.

How can I listen more attentively to the words of Christ?
In the decisions of life do I tend to build my house on rock, or on sand?
We pray for the courage to do the will of the Father.
We pray for those who endeavour to explain the good news to a
   reluctant world.

Tenth Sunday in Ordinary Time (Year A)

Matthew 9:9–13

As Jesus was walking on from there he saw a man named Matthew sitting at the tax office, and he said to him, 'Follow me.' And he got up and followed him. Now while he was at table in the house it happened that see, a number of tax collectors and sinners came to sit at the table with Jesus and his disciples. When the Pharisees saw this they said to his disciples, 'Why does your teacher eat with tax collectors and sinners?' When he heard this he replied, 'It is not the healthy who need a doctor, but the sick. Go and learn what this means, *My pleasure is in mercy, not sacrifice*. And indeed I came to call not the righteous, but sinners.'

Other readings: Hosea 6:3–6   Psalm 49 (50)   Romans 4:18–25

AFTER THE SERMON ON the Mount, the great discourse of Jesus at the beginning of the Gospel of Matthew, the evangelist records a series of miracles of Jesus. We then hear of the call of Matthew. It takes the classic form found in all the Synoptic Gospels (Mark, Matthew and Luke). The words 'Follow me!' invoke an immediate response from the disciple. But this time the occupation of the man who is called is the disreputable one of tax-collector. Tax-collectors colluded with oppressive rule and were often corrupt. For these reasons they were despised by the people.

The tax-collector Matthew, called Levi in the other gospels, is an unlikely choice to be a disciple. Not surprisingly, the gospel continues with reference to Jesus in the company of 'tax-collectors and sinners'. The story reaches a climax with the complaints of the Pharisees about Jesus sharing a meal with them.

The response of Jesus begins with what may be a proverb, that the sick, not the healthy, need a doctor. He then quotes a line from the prophet Hosea, taken from the passage which is in fact our first reading. The prophet invited people to show love as the first priority, before any concern for ritual sacrifices. The 'love' in the passage from Hosea embraces also the concept of 'mercy' in our gospel passage. Jesus comes to call sinners.

We also have quite an extensive reading from Paul's Letter to the Romans, which concerns the faith of Abraham. St Paul uses the example of Abraham to illustrate that salvation comes from faith, and not from doing good deeds. This topic has been much debated among Christians for centuries. We are saved by faith in the saving work of Christ, and not by any achievements of our own. Faith must then be lived out in works of love. What God asks of us is love and mercy.

Am I ready to leave everything as Matthew did to follow the call of Christ?

Do I feel unworthy to be involved in the things of God? What can I do about it?

Let us pray for those who cannot accept a God of love and mercy.

Let us pray for those who are considering a call to the priesthood or to the religious life.

Eleventh Sunday in Ordinary Time (Year A)

Matthew 9:36 – 10:8

And when he saw the crowds he felt sorry for them because they were harassed and dejected, like sheep without a shepherd. Then he said to his disciples, 'The harvest is rich but the labourers are few, so ask the Lord of the harvest to send out labourers to his harvest.'

He summoned his twelve disciples and gave them authority over unclean spirits, with power to drive them out and to cure every disease and every illness. These are the names of the twelve apostles: first, Simon who is known as Peter, and his brother Andrew; James the son of Zebedee, and his brother John; Philip and Bartholomew; Thomas, and Matthew the tax collector; James the son of Alphaeus, and Thaddaeus; Simon the Zealot and Judas Iscariot, who was also his betrayer. These twelve Jesus sent out, instructing them as follows:

'Do not go into gentile territory, and do not enter any Samaritan town; go instead to the lost sheep of the House of Israel. And as you go, proclaim that the kingdom of Heaven is close at hand. Cure the sick, raise the dead, cleanse the lepers, drive out demons. You received without charge, give without charge.'

Other readings: Exodus 19:2–6   Psalm 99 (100)   Romans 5:6–11

THE GOSPEL OF MATTHEW contains five major speeches of Jesus, designed by the evangelist, so it seems, to reflect and to outshine the five books of Moses. Jesus is the new Moses, who comes to bring the Law and the Prophets to fulfilment.

We hear today the beginning of the second speech, which is known as the Missionary Discourse. The opening words of our gospel passage tell us that the motivation of Jesus in his preaching is compassion for those who are lost. This must be our motivation too in offering the good news to others.

Jesus selects his twelve apostles. They are chosen from among those who have left everything to follow him. It may come as a surprise that with his first words to them Jesus apparently limits the mission of the apostles. The first priority of the mission must be the people of Israel, who are described as 'the lost sheep'. Later the mission will be extended to all the nations. The message is the one that Jesus has preached from the outset: 'The kingdom of heaven is near.' The message and the healings, which the disciples are to work in imitation of Jesus, are to be given freely.

Does my attitude to those who are lost imitate the compassion of Jesus?
Do I encourage and support those who are called to work for the
    spread of the gospel?
We pray that the Church may maintain its fidelity to the gospel of Jesus.
We pray that the Jewish people may be faithful to God's covenant.

Twelfth Sunday in Ordinary Time (Year A)

Matthew 10:26–33

Jesus said to the Twelve, 'So do not be afraid of them. Everything now covered up will be uncovered, and everything now hidden will be made clear. What I say to you in the dark, tell in the light; what you hear in whispers, proclaim from the housetops. Do not be afraid of those who kill the body but cannot kill the soul; fear him rather who can destroy both body and soul in hell. Are not two sparrows sold for a small coin? And yet not one of them falls to the ground without your Father. Of you, even the hairs on your head have been counted. So there is no need to be afraid; you are worth more than many sparrows. Everyone, therefore, who acknowledges me in the presence of others, I will acknowledge in the presence of my Father in heaven. But whoever denies me in the presence of others, I will deny in the presence of my Father in heaven.'

Other readings: Jeremiah 20:10–13   Psalm 68 (69)   Romans 5:12–15

WE CONTINUE READING THE Missionary Discourse of Jesus in the Gospel of Matthew. Jesus encourages the apostles to speak out and foresees the persecution of the missionaries. He urges the disciples to remember the providential love of God. In words reminiscent of the Sermon on the Mount, he points to the Father's care even for the well-being of sparrows.

At the same time he recognises that great courage is necessary to preach the gospel. It is not easy to shout the truth from the house-tops. It is not easy to declare oneself for Christ in the presence of those who ridicule and mock religion. The gospel reading invites us to ponder on the thousands of Christians who have spoken up for their faith at the risk of losing their lives, not only in distant centuries but also in our own day.

The first reading considers the words of Jeremiah who was persecuted for preaching the truth of God. He speaks of his distress, but also of his trust in the Lord who will protect him. The prophetic mission of Jeremiah and his fidelity amid suffering help us to understand the mission and suffering of Christ.

Our passage from the Letter to the Romans is of great significance. St Paul explains that while our first parents opened the gates for sin to enter into the world, the actions of Jesus Christ brought the free gift of life and salvation.

Do I have the courage to speak up for Christ when others mock my religion?
Do I trust in the providential care of the Father?
We pray for all those who speak up for the Christian message at the risk of their lives.
We pray for faith and courage amid all the difficulties of life.

Thirteenth Sunday in Ordinary Time (Year A)

Matthew 10:37–42

Jesus said to the Twelve, 'No one who prefers father or mother to me is worthy of me. No one who prefers son or daughter to me is worthy of me. Anyone who does not take the cross and follow in my footsteps is not worthy of me. Anyone who finds life will lose it; anyone who loses life for my sake will find it. Anyone who welcomes you welcomes me; and anyone who welcomes me welcomes the one who sent me. Anyone who welcomes a prophet as a prophet will have a prophet's reward; and anyone who welcomes a righteous person as a righteous person will have the reward of a righteous person. Anyone who gives so much as a cup of cold water to one of these little ones as a disciple, Amen I say to you, will most certainly not go without the reward.'

Other readings: 2 Kings 4:8–11, 14–16   Psalm 88 (89)   Romans 6:3–4, 8–11

THESE ARE THE CONCLUDING words of the Missionary Discourse of Jesus, the second of his major speeches in the Gospel of Matthew. Jesus challenges the disciples, and us too, to put no other person before our faith in him. For Christians there are new family ties, which, though not undermining our love of those dear to us, give us a broader perspective and a considerable challenge.

The cross is mentioned for the first time in Matthew's gospel, not the cross of Jesus, but the difficult burden that each one must bear in imitation of him. We are called to give our lives as Christ himself will give his life.

But the embrace of missionary discipleship offers us new joys. Those who offer a welcome to the disciples of Christ forge a relationship with Jesus, and with 'the one who sent him'. Friendships are transformed and offer us a wider and everlasting scope. How we treat others in this life, particularly the 'little ones', will bring us close to Jesus and to the one who sent him.

The first reading tells us how the prophet Elisha, centuries before Christ, received generous hospitality from a woman of Shunem. Her kindness is rewarded in an extraordinary way.

Do I place my faith in Jesus first in my life and relationships?
Am I willing to embrace my cross, whatever form it may take?
We pray for those who make great sacrifices in their service of the
*   gospel.*
We pray for generosity to the little ones of God.

Fourteenth Sunday in Ordinary Time (Year A)

Matthew 11:25–30

At that time Jesus exclaimed, 'I bless you, Father, Lord of heaven and of earth, for hiding these things from the wise and the clever and revealing them to infants. Yes, Father, for that was your good pleasure. Everything has been handed over to me by my Father; and no one knows the Son except the Father, nor does anyone know the Father except the Son and anyone to whom the Son chooses to reveal him. Come to me, all you who labour and are overburdened, and I will give you rest. Take my yoke upon you and learn from me, for I am gentle and humble in heart, and *you will find rest for your souls*. For my yoke is easy and my burden light.'

Other readings: Zechariah 9:9-10   Psalm 144 (145)   Romans 8:9, 11–13

OUR READING TODAY IS exclusively made up of the words of Jesus. The initial two verses are addressed to the Father, while in the remainder of the reading Jesus addresses his listeners. Both parts of the reading contain words of great beauty and great intimacy.

Jesus begins by praising the Father for allowing 'these things' to be known by those who, like children expectant of good things from loving parents, open their hearts and minds. In the previous passage in Matthew's gospel Jesus had condemned the refusal to repent of the lakeside towns. Despite the evidence of the mighty deeds and powerful preaching of Jesus their response was lukewarm.

Jesus rejoices in those whose hearts are open to receive and to learn. His next statement makes clear that he is the way to the Father. It is through knowing him that we come to know the Father. It is the Son alone who fully knows the Father and it is through the Son that those who are ready to receive and learn come to know the reality of God. These words may well remind us of some of the statements in John's gospel. 'It is the only Son, who is nearest the Father's heart, who has made God known.' (John 1:18)

No one can really listen to the final words of Jesus without being moved at the compassion of God. As the reading from the prophet Zechariah illustrates, the Messiah comes not to dominate and control but humbly to offer new life and strength.

We continue to read from St Paul's Letter to the Romans. Paul speaks of the Spirit who gives us life. The same Spirit who was revealed in power at the resurrection of Jesus gives new life to us in baptism. We are free to accept and live that new life. We are free to receive the good news like 'mere children' or to reject it and thereby lose the greatest gift.

Do I allow the life of God, Father, Son and Spirit, into my mind and heart?

Do I welcome and trust in the loving care of Jesus?

We pray for those who are overburdened with the problems of life.

We pray for the courage to take up the yoke of Christ and follow him.

Fifteenth Sunday in Ordinary Time (Year A)

Matthew 13:1–23

That same day Jesus left the house and sat by the lakeside, but such large crowds gathered round him that he got into a boat and sat there. The people all stood on the shore, and he told them many things in parables.

He said, 'Listen, a sower went out to sow. As he sowed, some seeds fell on the edge of the path, and the birds came and ate them up. Others fell on patches of rock where they found little soil and sprang up at once, because there was no depth of earth; but as soon as the sun came up they were scorched and, not having any roots, they withered away. Others fell among thorns, and the thorns grew up and choked them. Others fell on rich soil and produced their crop, some a hundredfold, some sixty, some thirty. Anyone who has ears should listen!'

Then the disciples went up to him and asked, 'Why do you talk to them in parables?' In answer, he said, 'Because to you it is granted to understand the mysteries of the kingdom of Heaven, but to them it is not granted. Anyone who has will be given more and will have more than enough; but anyone who has not will be deprived even of what he has. The reason

I talk to them in parables is that they look without seeing and listen without hearing or understanding. So in their case what was spoken by the prophet Isaiah is being fulfilled:

> *Listen and listen, but never understand!*
> *Look and look, but never perceive!*
> *This people's heart has grown coarse,*
> *their ears dulled, they have shut their eyes tight*
> *to avoid using their eyes to see, their ears to hear,*
> *their heart to understand,*
> *changing their ways and being healed by me.*

'But blessed are your eyes because they see, your ears because they hear! Amen I say to you, many prophets and righteous people longed to see what you see, and did not see it; to hear what you hear, and did not hear it.

'So hear the parable of the sower. When anyone hears the word of the kingdom without understanding, the Evil One comes and carries off what was sown in the heart: this is the seed sown on the edge of the path. The seed sown on patches of rock is someone who hears the word and welcomes it at once with joy. But such a person has no root deep down and does not last; should some trial come, or some persecution on account of the word, at once that person falls away. The seed sown in thorns is someone who hears the word, but the worry of the world and the lure of riches choke the word and so it produces nothing. And the seed sown in rich soil is someone who hears the word and understands it; this is the one who yields a harvest and produces in one case a hundredfold, in another sixty, in another thirty.'

Other readings: Isaiah 55:10–11   Psalm 64 (65)   Romans 8:18–23

ONE OF THE INTERESTING features of the Gospel according to Matthew is that it contains five extensive discourses of Jesus, the first of which is the Sermon on the Mount. The evangelist, it seems, has compiled these speeches to indicate that Jesus is a teacher greater than Moses. As Moses inspired the five books of the Pentateuch, Jesus leaves us in five speeches the new law of the gospel.

The central discourse in chapter 13 is a collection of the parables of Jesus. The parable of the Sower is the first parable, for it is all about hearing, about really listening, about responding and about bearing fruit.

Later in the chapter Jesus explains that the seed represents the 'word of the kingdom', and that it falls into different situations and suffers various fates. The obvious question is what kind of reception are we providing for God's word. The challenge is to produce a hundredfold, which in agricultural terms would be a fantastic, indeed impossible, yield.

The prophet Second Isaiah teaches us that the word from God carries out the will of God and succeeds in what it was sent to do. With the grace of Christ we can yield a harvest.

St Paul speaks to us once again from the Letter to the Romans about the process of giving birth which he observes in the whole of creation. Our lives may be marked by suffering and struggle, but we know from the life of Christ that this is the way to true life. It is by his grace that we reach 'the freedom and glory' of the children of God.

How do I react to 'the word of the kingdom'?

Am I able to see my sufferings as part of a process of being born to new life?

We pray for all those who sow the seed of the word, that they may do so with wisdom and love.

We pray for those who resist the attraction of the gospel.

Sixteenth Sunday in Ordinary Time (Year A)

Matthew 13:24–43

He put another parable before them, 'The kingdom of Heaven may be compared to a man who sowed good seed in his field. While everybody was asleep his enemy came, sowed darnel all among the wheat, and made off. When the new wheat sprouted and ripened, then the weeds appeared as well. The owner's servants went to him and said, "Sir, was it not good seed that you sowed in your field? If so, where do the weeds come from?" He said to them, "Some enemy has done this." And the servants said, "Do you want us to go and collect it in?" But he said, "No, because when you collect the weeds you might pull up the wheat with it. Let them both grow till the harvest, and at harvest time I shall say to the reapers: first collect the weeds and tie them in bundles to be burnt, then gather the wheat into my barn."'

He put another parable before them, 'The kingdom of Heaven is like a mustard seed which a man took and sowed in his field. It is the smallest of all the seeds, but when it has grown it is the biggest of shrubs and becomes a tree, so that the birds of the air come and shelter in its branches.'

He told them another parable, 'The kingdom of Heaven is like the yeast a woman took and mixed in with three measures of flour till it was leavened all through.' In all this Jesus spoke to the crowds in parables; indeed, he would never speak to them except in parables. This was to fulfil what was spoken by the prophet:

> I will open my mouth in parables,
> unfold what has been hidden since the foundation of
>   the world.

Then, leaving the crowds, he went to the house; and his disciples came to him and said, 'Explain to us the parable about the weeds in the field.' He said in reply, 'The sower of the good seed is the Son of man. The field is the world; the good seed is the subjects of the kingdom; the weeds, the subjects of the Evil One; the enemy who sowed them, the devil; the harvest is the end of the world; the reapers are the angels. Well then, just as the weeds are gathered up and burnt in the fire, so it will be at the end of time. The Son of man will send his angels and they will gather out of his kingdom all causes of stumbling and all who do evil, and throw them into the furnace of fire, where there will be weeping and gnashing of teeth. Then the righteous will shine like the sun in the kingdom of their Father. Anyone who has ears should listen!'

Other readings: Wisdom 12:13, 16–19   Psalm 85 (86)   Romans 8:26–27

ONCE AGAIN WE HAVE an extensive reading from Matthew chapter 13, in which the evangelist has gathered together the parables of Jesus. The parable of the weeds in the wheat is followed by the parable of the mustard seed, the parable of the yeast, and then Jesus' explanation of the parable of the weeds.

This particularly troublesome kind of weed resembles wheat. It can be easily understood why the land-owner instructs the labourers to remove the weed only at harvest-time, for to pull it out beforehand would probably uproot the wheat and thus destroy the crop. All this has implications for the lesson of the parable.

The kingdom of heaven on earth survives in the midst of a world which is tarnished by sin in its many forms. Christians have to work out how to cope and not collude with the reality of sin all around them. The parable also teaches that the time of the harvest will one day come, when God will take to himself those who have sought him by pursuing what is good and true, by living in faith, hope and love.

Matthew frequently speaks of the judgement to come. He gives a dramatic description of the Last Judgement in chapter 25 of his gospel. The wicked are consigned to the fires of hell, just as in this parable fire destroys the weeds. The fire should be understood as an image of the terrible pain that the loss of God involves. God does not inflict dreadful punishments on sinners, but those who reject what is good and true shut themselves off from the love of God and bring on themselves the terrible pain of the loss of God.

How do I cope with the evil I see around me?
Do I have the patience to wait for God's purposes to be fulfilled?
We pray for constancy in seeking what is good.
We pray for a true understanding of the forbearance of God.

Seventeenth Sunday in Ordinary Time (Year A)

Matthew 13:44–52

Jesus said to the crowds, 'The kingdom of Heaven is like treasure hidden in a field which someone has found; he hid it again, goes off in his joy, sells everything he owns and buys the field. Again, the kingdom of Heaven is like a merchant looking for fine pearls; when he found one of great value he went and sold everything he owned and bought it.

'Again, the kingdom of Heaven is like a dragnet cast in the sea and bringing in a haul of all kinds of fish. When it was full, they brought it ashore; then, sitting down, they collected the good ones in baskets and threw away the rotten ones. So it will be at the end of time: the angels will come out and separate the wicked from the righteous, to throw them into the blazing furnace, where there will be weeping and gnashing of teeth.

'Have you understood all these things?' They said to him, 'Yes.' And he said to them, 'Well then, every scribe instructed for the kingdom of Heaven is like a householder who brings out from his storeroom new things as well as old.'

Other readings: 1 Kings 3:5, 7–12   Psalm 118 (119)   Romans 8:28–30

THE LITURGY OF THE Word this Sunday celebrates the treasure we receive in the teaching which comes from God. Our gospel reading, from the chapter in which Matthew has collected many parables of Jesus, offers us three separate parables. Two of these, the treasure hidden in the field and the pearl of great price, provide rich images of the teaching of Jesus and what a great gift it is. The first reading, from the first Book of Kings, considers how king Solomon received the gift of a discerning heart from God. Jesus teaches with a wisdom which fulfils and surpasses the wisdom of Solomon.

The final parable, the dragnet cast into the sea, has similarities to the parable of the weeds in the field, which we heard last Sunday. The harvest from the sea contains both good and bad and these will only be separated at the judgement. Once again Matthew reminds us of the 'blazing furnace', symbolising the place where God can no longer be found. The anguish of the loss of God is expressed by the image of fire and in the phrase, 'there will be weeping and gnashing of teeth'.

The parable discourse of Jesus comes to an end with the question 'Have you understood?' The wise disciple of the kingdom of heaven treasures both what is newly discovered and what is old.

Do I consider the gospel preached by Jesus to be a unique treasure?
Do I seek wisdom and understanding as God's greatest gifts?
We pray for the wisdom truly to embrace and live the gospel of Jesus.
We pray for balance in dealing with what is new and what is old.

Eighteenth Sunday in Ordinary Time (Year A)

Matthew 14:13–21

When Jesus received this news he withdrew by boat to a lonely place on his own. But the crowds heard of this and, leaving the towns, went after him on foot. So as he stepped ashore he saw a large crowd; and he took pity on them and healed their sick.

When evening came, the disciples went to him and said, 'This is a lonely place, and time has slipped by; so send the people away, and they can go to the villages to buy themselves some food.' Jesus replied, 'There is no need for them to go: give them something to eat yourselves.' But they answered, 'All we have with us is five loaves and two fish.' So he said, 'Bring them here to me.'

He gave orders that the people were to sit down on the grass; then taking the five loaves and the two fish, and raising his eyes to heaven he said the blessing. And breaking the loaves he handed them to his disciples, who gave them to the crowds. They all ate as much as they wanted, and they collected the scraps left over, twelve baskets full. Now about five thousand men had eaten, to say nothing of women and children.

Other readings: Isaiah 55:1–3 Psalm 144 (145) Romans 8:35, 37–39

THE MULTIPLICATION OF THE loaves is perhaps the most renowned of all the extraordinary acts of Jesus which we call miracles, since it is found in all four gospels, and in both Matthew and Mark we find two separate accounts. The popularity of the tradition is surely due to the similarity between what Jesus does here and what he will do on the night before he dies: he takes the bread, he blesses it, he breaks it and he shares it.

The story can be understood in various ways. Matthew may have in mind that to provide bread for the crowds in 'a lonely place' is precisely what God did for the people who wandered with Moses through the desert. For Matthew, Jesus is a new Moses whose teaching and mighty acts surpass those of Moses himself. The story also speaks of Jesus as feeding the hungry, satisfying both material and spiritual need, and providing an example in not sending the people away, as the disciples had suggested.

Most powerfully, however, the story prepares us for the gift of himself which Jesus will give in death, which will be prefigured in the sharing of the last Passover meal. The Eucharist is for us the constant making present of the gift of Jesus to nourish us throughout our lives. 'Do this in memory of me,' said Jesus.

Do I endeavour to understand the deeper meaning of the miracles of Jesus?

How does the miracle of the loaves encourage me to value the gift of food?

We pray that the sharing of the Eucharist will teach us to share with those in need.

We pray for those who lack the basic requirements of life, and for a renewed commitment among world leaders to provide food for all.

Nineteenth Sunday in Ordinary Time (Year A)

Matthew 14:22–33

And at once he made the disciples get into the boat and go on ahead to the other side while he sent the crowds away. After sending the crowds away he went up into the hills on his own to pray. When evening came, he was there alone, while the boat, by now some furlongs from land, was hard pressed by rough waves, for there was a head-wind. Not long before dawn he came towards them, walking on the sea, and when the disciples saw him walking on the sea they were terrified. 'It is a phantom,' they said, and cried out in fear. But at once Jesus called out to them, saying, 'Courage! It's me! Don't be afraid.' Then Peter answered, saying, 'Lord, if it is you, tell me to come to you across the water.' Jesus said, 'Come!' Then Peter got out of the boat and started walking towards Jesus across the water, but noticing the wind, he took fright and as he began to sink cried out, 'Lord, save me!' Jesus put out his hand at once and held him. He said to him, 'You have so little faith; why did you doubt?' And as they got into the boat the wind dropped. The men in the boat worshipped him and said, 'Truly, you are Son of God.'

Other readings: 1 Kings 19:9, 11–13   Psalm 84 (85)   Romans 9:1–5

THREE OF THE GOSPEL writers, Matthew, Mark and John, give us an account of Jesus walking on the waters. It is an extraordinary miracle, which seems to be a manifestation of the power of Jesus. The Old Testament reading chosen to accompany this gospel is the revelation of God to Elijah in the 'sound of a gentle breeze', the 'still, small voice'. The evangelists place the story of the walking on the water directly after the multiplication of the loaves. Just as the loaves miracle reminds us of the provision of manna in the desert, the walking on the sea recalls God's power over the sea at the Exodus.

Matthew's account of the miracle has two special features. When he attempts to walk on the water, Peter is overcome with doubt and is upheld by Jesus. The gospel in which Peter is entrusted with authority also testifies to his vulnerability. In Matthew's version too the story ends with a declaration of faith by the disciples. While in Mark's version they remain confused and questioning, here they declare Jesus to be 'Son of God'. Matthew is surely indicating how Christians should understand this story.

In the reading from St Paul's Letter to the Romans Paul begins to speak about the situation of his Jewish brothers and sisters. He is profoundly grieved that they have not recognised Jesus as the promised Messiah. In the following sections of the letter Paul will explore and explain what God's intentions are in relation to the chosen people.

How do I react when my faith is tested by the storms of life?
Do I trust in the helping hand of the Lord when things are difficult?
We pray for confidence and serenity amid the trials of life.
We pray for the Jewish people that they may remain faithful to God's
   covenant.

Twentieth Sunday in Ordinary Time
(Year A)

Matthew 15:21–28

Jesus left that place and withdrew to the region of Tyre and Sidon. And suddenly out came a Canaanite woman from that district. She started shouting, 'Lord, son of David, have mercy on me. My daughter is tormented by a demon.' But he said not a word in answer to her. And his disciples went and pleaded with him, saying, 'Get rid of her, for she keeps shouting after us.' He said in reply, 'I was sent only to the lost sheep of the House of Israel.' But the woman had come up and worshipped him, saying, 'Lord, help me.' He replied, 'It is not right to take the children's food and throw it to dogs.' She said, 'Yes, Lord; but even dogs eat the scraps that fall from their masters' table.' Then Jesus answered her, 'Woman, great is your faith. Let your desire be granted.' And from that moment her daughter was well again.

Other readings: Isaiah 56:1, 6–7   Psalm 66 (67)   Romans 11:13–15, 29–32

ONE OF THE IMPORTANT issues in the ministry of Jesus is his attitude to foreigners, those who were not of the Jewish faith, known as 'Gentiles' or 'pagans'. The Gospel of Matthew is particularly keen to show that Jesus is the fulfilment of Jewish hopes. He is the Jewish Messiah. Earlier in the gospel, during the Missionary Discourse in chapter 10, Jesus had instructed his disciples to avoid the Gentiles and preach only to the 'lost sheep' of Israel. But Jesus has now entered the pagan region of Tyre and Sidon. When confronted with the Canaanite woman he ignores her and then affirms that his own mission is limited to Israel.

The persistence in faith of the pagan woman is sufficiently strong to obtain a healing for her daughter. We might ask why Jesus is so harsh with her. Is it simply that, knowing her faith, he tests her to express it? After all, earlier in the gospel, in chapter 8, Jesus had cured the servant of the Roman centurion and praised his faith.

The good news of the Kingdom is to be preached to all, but the initial priority of Jesus is to bring the gospel to his own people. The mission to the nations had already been hinted at in the visit of the magi from distant lands to the new-born child. It will be the mission of the Church to teach all nations, as the Risen Lord will make clear at the end of the Gospel of Matthew.

In the excerpt from the Letter to the Romans Paul declares that he has been made apostle to the nations. He is nevertheless convinced that it is God's purpose to bring his own Jewish brothers and sisters, as well as the pagans, to life in Christ. The faith of the nations will in time convince Israel that the God of all peoples has been revealed in Jesus Christ.

Is my faith resilient when I am faced with trials?
Do I rejoice in the faith of the nations which is displayed in the
    Catholic Church?
We pray that Christ's message of hope may reach all people.
We pray for the Jewish people that they may know the fulness of God's
    mercy.

Twenty-first Sunday in Ordinary Time (Year A)

Matthew 16:13–20

When Jesus came to the region of Caesarea Philippi he put this question to his disciples, 'Who do people say the Son of man is?' And they said, 'Some say John the Baptist, some Elijah, and others Jeremiah or one of the prophets.' He said to them, 'But you, who do you say I am?' In answer Simon Peter said, 'You are the Messiah, the Son of the living God.' In reply Jesus said to him, 'Blessed are you, Simon son of Jonah, for flesh and blood has not revealed this to you but my Father in heaven. So I now say to you: "You are Peter and on this rock I will build my church. And the gates of the underworld will never overpower it. I will give you the keys of the kingdom of Heaven: whatever you bind on earth will be bound in heaven; whatever you loose on earth will be loosed in heaven."' Then he instructed the disciples not to tell anyone that he was the Messiah.

Other readings: Isaiah 22:19–23   Psalm 137 (138)   Romans 11:33–36

ALL THE GOSPELS, AND the synoptic gospels (Mark, Matthew and Luke) in particular, witness to the growth in faith of the disciples of Jesus. In the synoptic gospels a point of climax is reached when Jesus asks his disciples the question: 'Who do you say I am?' It is a question which all Christians must answer.

Peter speaks up and declares his belief, perhaps also shared by the others, that Jesus is the promised Messiah. What is special in Matthew's story of Peter's profession of faith is the commissioning of Peter which follows. Faith leads to a mission.

The words of Jesus to Peter 'You are Peter, and on this rock I will build my Church' have been understood as the basis for the special role of the bishop of Rome, the successor of Peter, in relation to the whole church. In their varying ways each of the gospels testifies to the leadership role of Peter. The words of Jesus to Peter in Matthew's gospel are words of assurance, for it is Christ who will build the Church and Christ who endows Peter with authority.

The reading ends with Jesus instructing the disciples to tell nobody he was the Christ. The title of 'Christ' or 'Messiah' was understood in various ways, and Jesus had reservations that he might be misunderstood as a worldly leader. The true role of the Messiah will be taken up again in next Sunday's gospel reading.

In the second reading St Paul praises the providential wisdom of God.

What is the role of Jesus the Messiah in my understanding?
What does it mean to say that Jesus founded the Church?
We pray for the Pope that he may show the wisdom and love of Christ
*   in all his actions.*
We pray that the Church may be a place of welcome, hope and
*   encouragement for all.*

Twenty-second Sunday in Ordinary Time (Year A)

Matthew 16:21–27

From then onwards Jesus began to show his disciples that he must go to Jerusalem and suffer grievously at the hands of the elders and chief priests and scribes and to be put to death and to be raised up on the third day. Then, taking him aside, Peter began to rebuke him, saying, 'Heaven preserve you, Lord, this must not happen to you.' But he turned and said to Peter, 'Get behind me, Satan! You are a stumbling-block to me, because you are thinking not as God thinks but as humans do.'

Then Jesus said to his disciples, 'Anyone who wants to be a follower of mine must renounce self and take up the cross and follow me. For whoever wants to save life will lose it; but whoever loses life for my sake will find it. How does it profit someone to gain the whole world and forfeit life? Or what could anyone give in exchange for life? For the Son of man is going to come in the glory of his Father with his angels, and then he will reward each one according to behaviour. Amen I say to you, there are some standing here who will not taste death before they see the Son of man coming in his kingdom.'

Other readings: Jeremiah 20:7–9 Psalm 62 (63) Romans 12:1–2

LAST WEEK WE HEARD Peter's profession of faith in Jesus as the Messiah and the words spoken by Christ to Peter: 'You are Peter and on this rock I will build my church.' The conversation between Jesus and Peter continues in today's gospel and takes a very different turn. The suffering and death of Jesus will cast a shadow over the rest of the gospel.

Peter is shocked to hear Jesus speak for the first time of his approaching suffering, death and resurrection, shocked that the Messiah should suffer such a fate. Amid the differing opinions about God's Messiah, there was no expectation of suffering and death. Jesus himself, however, understood that the Messiah was also to be a 'suffering servant'.

The lesson for Peter is a lesson for all. Whatever our position in the Church we must be open to the unexpected ways of God, ready to learn new things, not to prefer 'man's way' to God's. The Christian is not called to position and prosperity in this world, but to self-sacrifice in the service of others. This is a constant challenge, which will often lead us on narrow and difficult paths. We can only face this reality knowing that Jesus has trodden the path before us, and that this road leads to the fulness of life.

The first reading, from one of the 'confessions' of the prophet Jeremiah, reveals the prophet's struggle and enduring commitment to preaching the word.

Am I open to the unexpected ways of God?
What are the crosses in my life that I refuse to carry willingly?
Let us pray for the courage and endurance we need in our Christian
    lives.
Let us pray for all who seek to alleviate the sufferings of others.

Twenty-third Sunday in Ordinary Time (Year A)

Matthew 18:15–20

Jesus said to his disciples, 'If your brother does something wrong, go and point out the fault between the two of you alone. If he listens to you, you have won back your brother. If he does not listen, take one or two others along with you, so that *the evidence of two or three witnesses is required to sustain the charge*. But if he refuses to listen to these, report it to the community; and if he refuses to listen to the community, treat him like a gentile or a tax collector. Amen I say to you, whatever you bind on earth will be bound in heaven; whatever you loose on earth will be loosed in heaven. Amen I say to you again, if two of you on earth agree on any matter, whatever you ask, it will be granted to you by my Father in heaven. For where two or three meet in my name, I am there among them.'

Other readings: Ezekiel 33:7–9   Psalm 94 (95)   Romans 13:8–10

THE GOSPEL OF MATTHEW contains five great speeches of Jesus, in which it appears that the evangelist has gathered together the teaching of Jesus on particular themes. Chapter 18 of the gospel contains the 'community discourse', which deals with issues relevant to the daily life of the church.

The question of correction of those who do wrong cannot be avoided. It is the responsibility of fellow-Christians to challenge and correct. The prophet Ezekiel deals with a similar issue: the responsibility of the prophet to confront wickedness. In both cases there is a need to speak the truth in difficult circumstances.

The gospel passage goes on to speak of the authority of the church to 'bind and loose', which is precisely the authority given to Peter earlier in his dialogue with Christ in chapter 16. Peter must always speak for and with the church, for and with the community of those who follow Christ. Finally, Jesus tells us of his presence when even two or three gather in his name. We are encouraged to listen to others before making decisions about the life of the church.

St Paul's words in the second reading are surely relevant here: 'Love is the one thing that cannot hurt your neighbour.' Love might be defined as acting for the real good of the other person. In dealing with sensitive issues in the life of the church love must always be the guide, but it is sometimes quite difficult to work out what love requires.

How can you know if and how to correct someone who has done wrong?

Can love of neighbour become an excuse for collusion?

Let us pray for wisdom and courage to confront difficult situations with both love and truth.

Let us pray for a deeper awareness of the presence of Christ when we gather in his name.

Twenty-fourth Sunday in Ordinary Time (Year A)

Matthew 18:21–35

Then Peter went up to him and said, 'Lord, how often must I forgive my brother or sister who wrongs me? As often as seven times?' Jesus answered, 'Not seven, I tell you, but seventy-seven times. And so the kingdom of Heaven may be compared to a king who decided to settle accounts with his servants. When he began the reckoning, someone was brought who owed him ten thousand talents; he had no means of paying, so his master gave orders that he should be sold, together with his wife and children and all his possessions, and payment made. So the servant threw himself down at his master's feet, with the words, "Be patient with me and I will pay you everything." And the servant's master felt so sorry for him that he let him go and cancelled the debt. Now on his way out the servant met one of his fellow-servants who owed him one hundred denarii; and he seized him and began to throttle him, saying, "Pay what you owe." His fellow-servant fell at his feet and appealed to him, saying, "Be patient with me and I will pay you." But the other would not agree; on the contrary, he threw him into prison till he should pay the debt. His fellow-servants were deeply distressed at what was happening, and they went and reported to their master everything that had happened. Then the master sent for the man and said to him, "You wicked servant, I cancelled all that debt of yours when you appealed to me. Were you not bound, then, to have pity on your fellow-servant just as I had pity on you?" And in his anger the master handed him over to the torturers till he should pay all his debt. And that is how my heavenly Father will deal with you unless you each forgive your brother and sister from your heart.'

**Other readings: Ecclesiasticus 27:30 – 28:7   Psalm 102 (103)
Romans 14:7–9**

JESUS' FOURTH GREAT SPEECH in the Gospel of Matthew, found in chapter 18 of the gospel, is the 'community discourse'. The final section of this speech is the lengthy parable of the unforgiving debtor, which is provoked by Peter's question about forgiveness.

What does it mean to forgive? The saying 'forgive and forget' is easily spoken but so difficult to implement. Many people feel confused by it. If someone has inflicted a profound wrong it is virtually impossible for the victim to forget, nor should he or she be expected to. But what about forgiving? Forgiving does not mean dismissing the evil committed or the hurt suffered. It is about not requiring a pay-back from the perpetrator, some kind of retribution, but rather seeking his or her forgiveness and healing. This is the hard challenge to follow Jesus in forgiving as he forgave as he hung on the cross. It is the challenge to behave not as human beings do but in imitation of the very mercy of God.

Is it possible to forgive and forget when the hurt is lasting and deep?
Is there someone to whom I can offer forgiveness in my heart today?
Let us pray for wisdom to understand that we are called to imitate
    God's compassion.
Let us pray for those whose lives are ruined by bitterness.

Twenty-fifth Sunday in Ordinary Time (Year A)

Matthew 20:1–16

Jesus said to his disciples, 'Now the kingdom of Heaven is like a landowner going out at daybreak to hire workers for his vineyard. He made an agreement with the workers for one denarius a day and sent them to his vineyard. Going out in mid-morning he saw others standing idle in the market place and said to them, "You go to the vineyard too and I will give you a fair wage." So they went. At about noon and again in mid-afternoon, he went out and did the same. Then not long before sunset he went out and found more men standing around, and he said to them, "Why have you been standing here idle all day?" They said to him, "Because no one has hired us." He said to them, "You go into the vineyard too." In the evening, the owner of the vineyard said to his manager, "Call the workers and pay them their wages, starting with the last and ending with the first." So those who were hired not long before sunset came forward and received one denarius each. When the first came they expected to get more, but they too received one denarius each. They took it, but grumbled at the landowner saying, "The men who came last have done only one hour, and you have treated them the same as us, though we have done a heavy day's work in all the heat." He answered one of them and said, "My friend, I am not being unjust to you; did we not agree on one denarius? Take your earnings and go. I choose to pay the last as much as I pay you. Is it not permissible for me to do what I like with my own? Or are you envious because I am generous?" Thus the last will be first, and the first, last.'

Other readings: Isaiah 55:6–9   Psalm 144 (145)   Philippians 1:20–24, 27

TODAY'S GOSPEL READING IS one of the parables of Jesus found only in the Gospel of Matthew. The parable of the Labourers in the Vineyard may give rise to some perplexity. Why does the landowner not pay the labourers according to the hours they have worked?

The parable is an invitation to understand that the ways of God are not bound or limited by human standards. The first reading, from the second part of the Book of Isaiah, is very well chosen to assist our understanding. God says: 'for my thoughts are not your thoughts, my ways not your ways'. God does not act according to the principles of human justice, whereby human beings are repaid according to their actions. God's loving generosity puts such considerations to one side.

The point of the parable is that we cannot demand rewards from God. The gifts which God bestows are always far greater than anything we can merit. We are saved not by our own efforts but by the boundless kindness of God which we gratefully welcome into our lives.

When has God taught you that the ways of God are different?
Is it appropriate to speak of the 'justice' of God?
We pray for openness to the things of God, which are beyond our full comprehension.
We pray for a spirit of forgiveness and acceptance of others.

Twenty-sixth Sunday in Ordinary Time (Year A)

Matthew 21:28–32

Jesus said, 'What do you think? A man had two sons. Going up to the first he said, "Son, go and work in the vineyard today." He answered, "I will not," but afterwards thought better of it and went. The man then went up to the second and said the same thing, and he answered, "I'll go, sir," but did not go. Which of the two did the father's will?' They said, 'The first.' Jesus said to them, 'Amen I say to you, tax collectors and prostitutes are going into the kingdom of God before you. For John came to you on the road of righteousness, but you did not believe him, and yet the tax collectors and prostitutes did. Even after seeing that, you refused to think better of it and believe in him.'

Other readings: Ezekiel 18:25–28   Psalm 24 (25)   Philippians 2:1–11

THE PARABLE OF THE Prodigal Son, found only in the Gospel of Luke, also features his elder brother. It is of course a very well-known parable. Matthew's parable about two sons, which is our gospel reading today, is less well-known.

There is an obvious contrast between the son who initially refuses to respond and then thinks better of it and does his father's bidding, and the second son who promises to respond but in fact does nothing. Jesus himself explains the parable.

The parable is apparently addressed to the chief priests and the elders. Jesus points out that many religious people pledge their loyalty in words but do not follow this up with actions. Jesus had spoken in the Sermon on the Mount about those who say 'Lord! Lord!', but do not do the will of the Father (7:21). Such people are contrasted with the tax collectors and prostitutes in the parable, who, after initially refusing to respond, change their lives for the better.

The first reading from the prophet Ezekiel makes clear that we are asked to do God's will and persevere in it. It may take a long time for us to accept the truth and challenge of the gospel, but God is patient and seems to prefer to await our free response rather than endure pious words which are not backed up by acts.

Jesus also reprimands the religious leaders for their blindness. Even when they saw the tax-collectors and sinners responding to the preaching of John the Baptist, they still refused to change themselves. Jesus will later accuse the religious leaders of blindness and hypocrisy: 'Alas for you, blind guides!' (23:16)

Am I blind to the example of those I consider to be not as good as I am?
Am I willing to turn over a new leaf despite past failings?
We pray that we may respect the efforts of others even if they fail.
We pray for insight and understanding of ourselves and of our
* neighbour.*

Twenty-seventh Sunday in Ordinary Time (Year A)

Matthew 21:33–43

Jesus said, 'Listen to another parable. There was a man, a landowner, who planted a vineyard; he fenced it round, dug a winepress in it and built a tower; then he leased it to tenants and went abroad. When vintage time drew near he sent his servants to the tenants to collect his produce. But the tenants seized his servants, thrashed one, killed another and stoned a third. Next he sent some more servants, this time a larger number, and they dealt with them in the same way. Finally he sent his son to them, thinking, "They will respect my son." But when the tenants saw the son, they said among themselves, "This is the heir. Come on, let us kill him and get his inheritance." So they seized him and threw him out of the vineyard and killed him. Now when the owner of the vineyard comes, what will he do to those tenants?' They answered, 'He will bring those wretches to a wretched end and lease the vineyard to other tenants who will deliver the produce to him at the proper time.' Jesus said to them, 'Have you never read in the scriptures:

The stone which the builders rejected
has become the cornerstone;
this is the Lord's doing
and it is amazing in our eyes?

'I tell you, then, that the kingdom of God will be taken from you and given to a people who will produce its fruit.'

Other readings: Isaiah 5:1–7   Psalm 79 (80)   Philippians 4:6–9

THE PROPHETS FREQUENTLY COMPARED the people of Israel to a vineyard. The prophet Isaiah, in today's first reading, speaks of the vineyard cherished by the Lord which produces only sour fruit. Jesus takes this parable of Isaiah as his starting-point.

Instead of placing the emphasis on the quality of the grapes produced in the vineyard, Jesus speaks of the tenants of the vineyard who refuse to give the landowner his produce. The tenants abuse the servants of the landowner and eventually kill the landowner's son.

Jesus is now in Jerusalem and he directs these words to those in authority, who, like many of their forefathers, do not heed the messengers of God and fail to produce a harvest of good works for God. It was principally the religious leaders who rejected the message of Jesus. In spite of this behaviour of some of the leaders of Judaism in Jesus' day, Christians still cherish the Jewish roots of our faith, and value the Old Testament and the Jewish traditions of Jesus and his gospel.

This parable contains a warning to listen and to respond, to 'produce the fruit of the kingdom'. Once again in this gospel the evangelist points to the receptivity of the Gentiles 'who will produce the fruit' of the kingdom. The Church of Christ welcomes all those who heed the message, both Jew and Gentile.

Do I endeavour to bear fruit in response to the gospel message?
Do I treasure the traditions of my faith, both its Jewish roots
*   and Christian fulfilment?*
We pray for wisdom and humility among the leaders of our
*   faith.*
We pray that the mission of the Church may prosper throughout
*   the world.*

Twenty-eighth Sunday in Ordinary Time (Year A)

Matthew 22:1–14

Jesus began to speak to them in parables once again, 'The kingdom of Heaven may be compared to a king who gave a feast for his son's wedding. He sent his servants to call those who had been invited, but they would not come. Next he sent some more servants with the words, "Tell those who have been invited: Look, I have prepared my banquet, my oxen and fattened cattle have been slaughtered, everything is ready. Come to the wedding." But they were not interested: one went off to his farm, another to his business, and the rest seized his servants, maltreated them and killed them. The king was furious. He despatched his troops, destroyed those murderers and burnt their town. Then he said to his servants, "The wedding is ready; but as those who were invited were not worthy, go to the main crossroads and invite to the wedding everyone you can find." So these servants went out onto the roads and collected together everyone they could find, bad and good alike; and the wedding hall was filled with guests. When the king came in to look at the guests he noticed one man who was not wearing a wedding garment, and said to him, "How did you get in here, my friend, without a wedding garment?" And the man was silent. Then the king said to the attendants, "Bind him hand and foot and throw him into the darkness outside, where there will be weeping and gnashing of teeth." For many are invited but few are chosen.'

Other readings: Isaiah 25:6–10 Psalm 22 (23) Philippians 4:12–14, 19–20

THE PARABLE WE HEAR today takes up the image of the feast of the kingdom of heaven. The theme of the banquet of eternal life runs through our readings today. The prophet Isaiah speaks of the day when all will be united at the feast provided by God. Our psalm reminds us of the Lord who prepares a banquet for each one. Jesus, who welcomed the unwanted and ate and drank with them during his earthly life, gives this parable of the wedding feast as a symbol of the life of the kingdom.

The reluctance of so many to come to the wedding speaks of

people who are immersed in the things of the world and have no time for the things of God. We can make many excuses for not responding to God's call. The invitation is extended to all, 'bad and good alike'. There is a constant need to respond to God's invitation, and make changes in our lives.

In the final verses of the parable there is a dramatic change of tone. Why is the man without the wedding garment thrown out? It seems to contradict the generosity of the earlier invitation to all. God's invitation is indeed directed to all, but there is always need of a deliberate response. To be carried along by the crowd without understanding where we are going is as bad as refusing the invitation in the first place!

Do I allow my daily preoccupations to take precedence over the search to find God?

Do I take my faith for granted without really trying to grow in knowledge and love of God?

We thank God for inviting us into communion with him.

We thank God for the sacraments, particularly the Holy Eucharist.

Twenty-ninth Sunday in Ordinary Time (Year A)

Matthew 22:15–21

Then the Pharisees went away to work out between them how to trap him in what he said. And they sent their disciples to him, together with the Herodians, to say, 'Master, we know that you are an honest man and teach the way of God in all honesty, and that you are not afraid of anyone, because human rank means nothing to you. What do you think? Is it permissible to pay taxes to Caesar or not?' But Jesus, aware of their malice, replied, 'You hypocrites! Why are you putting me to the test? Show me the coin for the tribute.' They handed him a denarius, and he said, 'Whose portrait is this? Whose title?' They replied, 'Caesar's.' Then he said to them, 'So pay Caesar what belongs to Caesar – and God what belongs to God.'

Other readings: Isaiah 45:1, 4–6   Psalm 95 (96)   1 Thessalonians 1:1–5

IN OUR READING OF the Gospel of Matthew we continue to hear of incidents during the ministry of Jesus in Jerusalem in the time leading up to his death and resurrection. There is an atmosphere of foreboding. There are plots to trap Jesus in order to bring charges against him. Jesus repeatedly reprimands the Jewish leaders for their unwillingness to listen to him.

The Pharisees attempt to 'trap Jesus in what he said'. The issue is that of the rightness of paying taxes. Palestine was under the rule of the Roman empire. Was it right to pay taxes to this pagan power machine? The question is like those asked of politicians and church leaders today to try to get them to give simple answers to complex questions. Jesus throws the question back to the questioners. He knows that the intention is to catch him out and does not engage in any debate.

Jesus' response is: 'Pay Caesar what belongs to Caesar, and God what belongs to God.' As Christians we cannot cut ourselves off from the affairs of the world, but we should never compromise our beliefs and values. Our decisions and our loyalties must be decided by what furthers the 'common good'.

Today we begin to read from the earliest letter of St Paul in the New Testament, the first letter to the Thessalonians. Paul assures the community that he remembers them in his prayers. The unity of the church, made up of local communities, is built up above all through prayer. Paul goes on to praise the people of this community for their active faith, their works of love and their perseverance in hope. The impact of the good news on them has been dramatic. The Holy Spirit has transformed their lives.

Do I have the patience to reflect on complex questions so that my actions may be for the good of all?

Am I willing to listen to the teaching of Jesus, especially when my actions are challenged?

We pray that we may always show honesty and truth in our dealings with others.

We pray that our lives will be full of faith, hope and love.

Thirtieth Sunday in Ordinary Time (Year A)

Matthew 22:34–40

But when the Pharisees heard that he had silenced the Sadducees they got together and, to put him to the test, one of them, a lawyer, put a further question, 'Master, which is the greatest commandment in the Law?' Jesus said to him, 'You shall love the Lord your God with all your heart, and with all your soul, and with all your mind. This is the greatest and the first commandment. The second is like it: You shall love your neighbour as yourself. On these two commandments hang the whole Law, and the Prophets.'

Other readings: Exodus 22:20–26   Psalm 17 (18)   1 Thessalonians 1:5–10

JESUS' DISCUSSIONS WITH THE religious leaders in Jerusalem continue in this gospel passage. The question about the law is asked according to this evangelist in order to 'put Jesus to the test'. The reply is Jesus' own summary of what the law of God requires, and it has become accepted as a brief expression of the whole moral law. His reply leaves them without anything to say.

If we return to the ancient expression of the law of God in the Ten Commandments we find no explicit reference to love of God and love of neighbour. Jesus draws together all the commandments under these two headings. What does Jesus mean by love? Love of God is our grateful response to the love shown by God throughout the history of salvation.

Love of neighbour is illustrated in our first reading, from the book of Exodus, with its explicit instructions from the law about caring for those in need, the stranger, the widow, the orphan. Our actions must be guided by concern for the real good of others, and an awareness of their needs.

We may notice that Jesus does not refer to the love he himself shows. It is not until the Gospel of John, with its profound reflection on the actions of Jesus, that we hear Jesus saying: 'Love one another as I have loved you.' (John 13:34) It is in his self-giving death on the cross that his love comes to a climax. This supreme act of love is the model for the love Christians must show. The love shown by the Son of God in going to his death, which is present for us in the Eucharist, draws us into deeper love, for God and for neighbour.

St Paul continues in the first letter to the Thessalonians to praise their Christian witness. Their lives, which have been renewed by faith, have drawn others to the gospel. 'The news of your faith in God has spread everywhere!' writes Paul. They now live in expectation of the return of the risen Christ.

Do I attempt to follow Christ's commands of love in my daily life?
Do I endeavour to imitate in some way the self-giving love of Christ?
We thank God for the new law of love.
We pray for all Christians whose example gives us encouragement.

Thirty-first Sunday in Ordinary Time (Year A)

Matthew 23:1–12

Then addressing the crowds and his disciples Jesus said, 'The scribes and the Pharisees occupy the chair of Moses. You must therefore do and observe everything that they tell you; but do not do what they do, since they do not practise what they teach. They tie up heavy burdens and lay them on people's shoulders, but they do not lift a finger to move them. Everything they do is done to be seen by others, for they make their headbands broader and their tassels longer. They love the place of honour at banquets and the front seats in the synagogues, and greetings in the market squares and to be addressed by people as Rabbi. You, however, must not allow yourselves to be called Rabbi, since you have only one Master, and you are all brothers and sisters. You must call no one on earth your father, since you have only one Father, and he is in heaven. Nor must you allow yourselves to be called teachers, for you have only one Teacher, the Messiah. The greatest among you will be your servant. Anyone who raises himself up will be humbled, and anyone who humbles himself will be raised up.'

Other readings: Malachi 1:14 – 2:2, 8–10   Psalm 130 (131)
1 Thessalonians 2:7–9, 13

THIS CHAPTER OF THE Gospel according to Matthew is notable for the strong verbal attacks of Jesus on the scribes and Pharisees. To our shame the words of Jesus in this chapter have been used in the past to encourage hatred of the Jews. In modern times the Church has made it abundantly clear that Christians should treasure their relationship with the Jewish people, who have rightly been called 'our elder brothers and sisters in faith'.

In every age, and probably in every religion, religious leadership has gone astray and failed to live up to high ideals. Today's words from the prophet Malachi accuse the priests of straying from the true path and causing many to stumble.

We need religious leaders to guide and direct us, but, as in the days of Jesus, religious leaders can be seduced by status. They can covet places of honour and elaborate vestments. Christians leaders can lose sight of the example of Christ.

Jesus' example is one of humble service. He is the true rabbi, teacher and master. All of us are called to follow in humility the one who came to serve and to make our journey with him towards the fulness of God's life.

Do I take inappropriate pride in the trappings of my Christian life?
Am I ready to humble myself, and is my spirit truly dedicated to Christ?
We pray for religious leaders that they may behave with sincerity and integrity at all times.
We pray for those who are led astray by status and pomposity.

Thirty-second Sunday in Ordinary Time (Year A)

Matthew 25:1–13

Jesus said, 'Then the kingdom of Heaven will be like ten girls who took their lamps and went to meet the bridegroom. Five of them were foolish and five were wise. The foolish ones took their lamps, but took no oil with them, whereas the wise ones took flasks of oil as well as their lamps. The bridegroom delayed, and they all grew drowsy and fell asleep. But at midnight there was a cry, "Look! The bridegroom! Go out and meet him." Then all those girls woke up and trimmed their lamps, and the foolish ones said to the wise ones, "Give us some of your oil: our lamps are going out." But they replied, "There may not be enough for us and for you; you had better go to the oil-sellers and buy some for yourselves." They had gone off to buy it when the bridegroom arrived. Those who were ready went in with him to the wedding hall and the door was closed. The other girls arrived later, saying, "Lord, Lord, open the door for us." But he replied, "Amen I say to you, I do not know you." So stay awake, because you do not know either the day or the hour.'

Other readings: Wisdom 6:12–16   Psalm 62 (63)   1 Thessalonians 4:13–18

THIS PARABLE, UNIQUE TO the Gospel of Matthew, is one section of the fifth and final great speech of Jesus, which considers the end of the world and the gathering together of God's people. This final speech also contains the great drama of the judgement: 'Whenever you did this to the least of my brothers and sisters you did it to me.'

This parable is full of symbols. Jesus is described as the bridegroom repeatedly in the four gospels. Earlier in this gospel (9:15), in a reference to his passion and death, he spoke of himself as 'the bridegroom who will be taken away'.

This image has its origins in the Jewish Scriptures, where the relationship of the people to God was compared to that of a bride to her husband. The Church, the new people of God, is rightly described as the bride of Christ. It is our role to accompany and serve the bridegroom. We all take on this task from the time of our baptism. But will we be ready when the bridegroom appears?

The symbol of the lamp brings an even clearer allusion to Christian life and to the sacrament of baptism. We receive the light of Christ when we are baptised, and we are constantly challenged to keep the light burning brightly. This responsibility is reflected in the determination of the wise girls not to let their lamps go out. The foolish girls, on the other hand, have allowed themselves to be distracted from what is really important in their lives.

Do I see my life as a preparation to meet the Lord?
Do I nourish my life with prayer and the sacraments?
We pray for those who have lost their way on the journey of life.
We ask for a deeper appreciation of the gifts the Lord bestows on us.

Thirty-third Sunday in Ordinary Time (Year A)

Matthew 25:14–30

Jesus said to his disciples, 'It is like a man about to go abroad who summoned his servants and entrusted his property to them. To one he gave five talents, to another two, to a third one, each in proportion to his ability. Then he set out on his journey. The man who had received the five talents promptly went and traded with them and made five more. The man who had received two made two more in the same way. But the man who had received one went off and dug a hole in the ground and hid his master's money. Now a long time afterwards, the master of those servants came and settled accounts with them. The man who had received the five talents came forward bringing five more and saying, "Sir, you entrusted me with five talents; here are five more that I have made." His master said to him, "Well done, good and trustworthy servant; you have been trustworthy in small things; I will put you in charge of many; come and join in your master's joy." Next the man with the two talents came forward, saying, "Sir, you entrusted me with two talents; here are two more that I have made." His master said to him, "Well done, good and trustworthy servant; you have been trustworthy in small things; I will put you in charge of many; come and join in your master's joy." Last came forward the man who had the single talent, saying, "Sir, I knew you were a hard man, reaping where you had not sown and gathering where you had not scattered; so I was afraid, and I went off and hid your talent in the ground. Here, take what is yours." But his master answered him, "You wicked and lazy servant! You knew that I reap where I have not sown and gather where I have not scattered? You should have deposited my money with the bankers, and on my return I would have got my money back with interest. So now, take the talent from him and give it to the man who has the ten talents. For to everyone who has, more will be given, and there will be more than enough; but anyone who has not, will be deprived even of what he has. As for this useless servant, throw him into the darkness outside, where there will be weeping and gnashing of teeth.'"

Other readings: Proverbs 31:10–13, 19–20, 30–31   Psalm 127 (128) 1 Thessalonians 5:1–6

THE PARABLE OF THE talents comes in the last of the five major speeches of Jesus in the Gospel of Matthew. The focus is on the end of time and the question of how we have used our talents.

As we draw towards the end of the liturgical year these are the questions which the liturgy inspires. Next week we shall hear how the discourse continues with Jesus' description of the judgement. Ultimately, we shall all be judged on love.

Am I grateful for the gifts and opportunities given me?
Do I use my talents, whatever they are, to live out the commandment of love?
We pray for acceptance of who we are and the generosity to give whatever we have.
We thank God for the example of self-giving of Jesus.

Christ the King (Year A)

Matthew 25:31–46

Jesus said to his disciples, 'When the Son of man comes in his glory, escorted by all the angels, then he will take his seat on his throne of glory. All nations will be assembled before him and he will separate them from one another as the shepherd separates sheep from goats. He will place the sheep on his right hand and the goats on his left. Then the King will say to those on his right hand, "Come, you that are blessed by my Father, inherit the kingdom prepared for you since the foundation of the world. For I was hungry and you gave me food, I was thirsty and you gave me drink, I was a stranger and you welcomed me, needing clothes and you clothed me, sick and you visited me, in prison and you came to see me." Then the righteous will say to him in reply, "Lord, when did we see you hungry and feed you, or thirsty and give you drink? When did we see you a stranger and welcome you, needing clothes and we clothed you? When did we see you sick or in prison and go to you?" And the King will answer, "Amen I say to you, in so far as you did this to one of the least of these brothers or sisters of mine, you did it to me." Then he will say to those on his left hand, "Go away from me, accursed, to the eternal fire prepared for the devil and his angels. For I was hungry and you did not give me food, I was thirsty and you did not give me anything to drink, I was a stranger and you did not welcome me, needing clothes and you never clothed me, sick and in prison and you did not visit me." Then they in their turn will ask, "Lord, when did we see you hungry or thirsty, a stranger or needing clothes, sick or in prison, and did not come to your aid?" Then he will answer, "Amen I say to you, in so far as you neglected to do this to one of the least of these, you neglected to do it to me." And they will go away to eternal punishment, and the righteous to eternal life.'

**Other readings: Ezekiel 34:11–12, 15–17   Psalm 22 (23)
1 Corinthians 15:20–26, 28**

ON THIS FINAL SUNDAY of the liturgical year, the Solemnity of Christ the King, we come to the end of our reading of the Gospel according to Matthew. The dramatic scene of the judgement comes at the end of the fifth and last major speech of Jesus in this gospel, a speech which is focused on the final coming of the kingdom.

In this passage, which is both an invitation and a warning, Jesus is presented as 'the King'. He has dominion over all. He is the judge, but the needy of the world are his brothers and sisters. We are invited to loving service of our brothers and sisters, especially of those in greatest need. The dreadful fate of 'eternal punishment' is the inevitable consequence of a refusal to love. It is only this deliberate refusal to love that can exclude us from the kingdom.

Do you see this gospel text as an encouragement or as a warning?
What lessons have you learned from hearing the Gospel of Matthew this year?
We pray for our young people, that they may respond with generosity to God's call in their lives.
We pray that the gospel will be the motivating force in our lives, year by year.

SUNDAYS IN ORDINARY TIME

YEAR B

Second Sunday in Ordinary Time (Year B)

John 1:35–42

The next day John was again standing there with two of his disciples, and looking at Jesus walking by he said, 'Look, there is the lamb of God.' And the two disciples heard him speaking and followed Jesus. Jesus turned round, and seeing them following said, 'What are you looking for?' They answered, 'Rabbi,' – which translated means Teacher – 'where are you staying?' He said to them, 'Come and see'; so they went and saw where he was staying, and stayed with him that day. It was mid-morning. One of these two who had heard John speak and had followed him was Andrew, the brother of Simon Peter. He first found his brother Simon and said to him, 'We have found the Messiah' – which is translated Christ – and he took Simon to Jesus. Jesus looked at him and said, 'You are Simon, son of John; you shall be called Cephas' – which means Rock.

Other readings: 1 Samuel 3:3–10, 19   Psalm 39 (40)
1 Corinthians 6:13–15, 17–20

OUR READING THIS SUNDAY is taken from the later verses of the first chapter of John, which is generally read during the Christmas season. These verses cover the early days of the ministry of Jesus. We have a last glimpse of John the Baptist, who heralds Jesus for a second time as 'the Lamb of God'. Jesus is the one who is to lay down his life like an innocent lamb 'for the sins of the world'. This is the purpose of his coming into the world, the purpose of the Son of God 'becoming flesh' and 'living among us'.

Attention quickly moves away from John the Baptist to the conversation between Jesus and the two disciples. They follow Jesus, but he challenges them with the question 'what are you looking for?'

They counter this question with another, 'where are you staying?' Jesus invites them: 'Come and see!'

The time they spend with Jesus makes a deep impression on them. Andrew cannot contain his enthusiasm. He is convinced that Jesus is the Christ, the Messiah. He calls his brother Simon Peter. When Jesus meets Simon Peter, he does not hesitate to enlist him among the disciples and immediately gives him the new name, Cephas, which means Rock.

These verses are marked by the enthusiastic response of the first disciples to Jesus and their eagerness to spread the news about him. This eagerness is an echo of the first reading, in which Samuel is called as a boy to be a prophet. When the good news of salvation comes, when the encounter with the word of God arrives, it cannot be contained or suppressed. It is imperative to let others know!

'What are you looking for?' What would be your response to Jesus' question?

How often do you invite others to 'come and see' something of your life of faith?

We pray that, as another year begins, we may meet Jesus with new enthusiasm.

Let us have the courage to make Jesus known to others, as the first disciples did.

Third Sunday in Ordinary Time (Year B)

Mark 1:14–20

After John had been arrested, Jesus went into Galilee, proclaiming the gospel from God and saying, 'The time is fulfilled, and the kingdom of God has drawn near. Repent and believe in the gospel.'

As he was walking along by the Lake of Galilee he saw Simon and Simon's brother Andrew casting a net in the lake – for they were fishermen. And Jesus said to them, 'Come after me and I will make you fishers of people.' And at once, leaving their nets, they followed him.

Going on a little further, he saw James son of Zebedee and his brother John; they too were in their boat, mending the nets. At once he called them and, leaving their father Zebedee in the boat with the hired men, they went after him.

Other readings: Jonah 3:1–5, 10   Psalm 24 (25)   1 Corinthians 7:29–31

THIS SUNDAY WE BEGIN our reading of the gospel laid down to be read on Ordinary Sundays this year, the Gospel according to Mark, the first and the shortest of the four gospels.

Mark begins his gospel without any reference to the birth or early life of Jesus. A short account of the ministry of John the Baptist is followed by the story of the baptism of Jesus and a brief reference to his temptation in the desert. Our passage begins with Jesus in Galilee proclaiming the 'good news' or 'gospel' of God. Jesus declares the coming of 'the time' and of 'the kingdom of God'. The essence of his preaching is that the time of fulfilment, the long-awaited time, has arrived. God's kingdom, God's rule, is coming. The power of evil and of sin will be challenged, and overcome. This will be the constant theme of the words and deeds of Jesus in Mark. The first half of the gospel is set mostly in the northern region of Galilee. It is here that the gospel is first heard and first welcomed.

Our reading continues with the call of the first disciples. They are taken away abruptly from their daily work of fishing. They respond immediately to Jesus' summons. They do not show the reluctance which Jonah showed (first reading). The call of Jesus is irresistible. We learn the names of the first four disciples, the brothers Simon and Andrew, and the brothers James and John. They abandon both their work, and their family ties. Something momentous is happening in their lives. It is amid the preoccupations of each day that the Lord calls his disciples, and calls them by name.

What was it like when you first understood and welcomed the message of the good news?

What has been your response to the call of Jesus at times of crisis or turning points in life?

On this Sunday of the Word of God we pray for a deeper appreciation of the good news of Jesus.

We pray for an understanding that only through God's goodness can our lives be free from worry and full of happiness.

Fourth Sunday in Ordinary Time (Year B)

Mark 1:21–28

They went into Capernaum, and at once on the Sabbath he went into the synagogue and began to teach. And they were amazed at his teaching, because he taught them with authority, not like the scribes.

And at once in their synagogue there was a man with an unclean spirit, and he cried out saying, 'What do you want with us, Jesus of Nazareth? Have you come to destroy us? I know who you are: the Holy One of God.' And Jesus rebuked it saying, 'Be quiet! Come out of him!' And the unclean spirit threw the man into convulsions and with a loud cry went out of him. All the people were so astonished that they started asking one another what it meant, saying, 'A new teaching, with authority: he gives orders even to unclean spirits and they obey him.' And his reputation at once spread everywhere, through all the surrounding Galilean countryside.

**Other readings: Deuteronomy 18:15–20   Psalm 94 (95)
1 Corinthians 7:32–35**

AFTER THE CALL OF the first disciples, the evangelist tells us of a healing worked by Jesus, the first miracle in this gospel. He reaches Capernaum, a busy town by the Sea of Galilee, which he made the centre for his ministry. His teaching impressed the people, for it was given with authority, with conviction. Jesus spoke the truth without fear. The people are even more astonished by the healing of the man who was 'possessed by an unclean spirit'.

The initial part of the gospel is dominated by the words and the actions of Jesus. The healing actions show the power of God, while the teaching proclaims the coming of the kingdom. Jesus' powerful deeds confirm the message of the coming of the kingdom of God.

The sick man was probably suffering from some kind of mental illness, and considered to be 'possessed'. All sickness was considered evil and in some way the work of Satan. The sick man was somehow a victim of evil. By healing him Jesus challenges and conquers the power of Satan. He demonstrates that the kingdom is near.

The reading from the book of Deuteronomy includes the words
of Moses that God would one day raise up a great prophet, a prophet
like Moses. This reading prepares us for the gospel reading and the
fulfilment of that promise. Jesus, who is greater than Moses, speaks
powerful words, words of truth, words which heal. The good news
Jesus brings can change our lives as it changed the life of the sick
man in the gospel.

What does this gospel say to us today?
What does the gospel tell us about sickness?
Let us pray for all those who care for the sick and work for their
*   healing.*
Let us pray for those who preach the gospel that they may do so
*   with courage and love.*

Fifth Sunday in Ordinary Time (Year B)

Mark 1:29–39

And at once on leaving the synagogue, he went with James
and John into the house of Simon and Andrew. Now Simon's
mother-in-law was lying there feverish, and at once they told
him about her. He went to her, took her by the hand and
raised her up. And the fever left her and she began to serve
them.

That evening, after sunset, they brought to him all who
were sick and those who were possessed by demons. The
whole town was gathered together at the door, and he cured
many who were sick with diseases of one kind or another;
he also drove out many demons, but he would not allow the
demons to speak, because they knew who he was.

In the morning, while it was still deep in the night, he
went out and left the house and went off to a lonely place and
prayed there. Simon and his companions set out in search
of him, and when they found him they said, 'Everybody is
looking for you.' He answered, 'Let us go elsewhere, to the
neighbouring villages, so that I can proclaim the message
there too, because that is why I came.' And he went all through

Galilee, proclaiming the message in their synagogues and driving out demons.

Other readings: Job 7:1–4, 6–7   Psalm 146 (147)
1 Corinthians 9:16–19, 22–23

AS HE BEGINS THE story of the ministry of Jesus, Mark sets before us a typical day's ministry of Jesus in Capernaum. It begins with the healing of the sick man in the synagogue, which we read last week. There are many others who also need Jesus' help.

Jesus is still accompanied by the four disciples, the first ones to be called. The evangelist tells us how he heals the mother-in-law of Simon Peter. Jesus 'raised her up'. This is the term used for the resurrection of Jesus. The miracles of Jesus are signs of the kingdom, and point to the resurrection. He has come to raise up to new life those who welcome his help.

At sunset, once the sabbath has ended, the townspeople begin to bring their sick to Jesus. Mark stresses the impact of Jesus' healing work by speaking of the gathering of the 'whole town'. There is another reference to those who are possessed, those who in the contemporary view were victims of Satan. Jesus commands them not to make him known. He is constantly concerned to avoid any misunderstanding of his mission and purpose.

The evangelist brings the day to a conclusion by speaking of Jesus at prayer before the night ends.

How do I experience the new life and healing Jesus brings?
Do I allow time for quiet prayer in my daily life?
Let us pray for those who struggle with debilitating sickness of body
    or spirit.
Let us pray for those who care for sick and elderly family members.

Sixth Sunday in Ordinary Time (Year B)

Mark 1:40–45

A leper came to him and pleaded on his knees saying, 'If you are willing, you can cleanse me.' Moved with pity, Jesus stretched out his hand, touched him and said to him, 'I am willing. Be cleansed.' And at once the leprosy left him and he was cleansed. And at once Jesus sternly sent him away and said to him, 'See that you say nothing to anyone, but go and show yourself to the priest, and make the offering for your cleansing prescribed by Moses as evidence to them.' The man went away, but then started freely proclaiming and telling the story everywhere, so that Jesus could no longer go openly into any town, but stayed outside in deserted places. But people from everywhere kept coming to him.

Other readings: Leviticus 13:1–2, 44–46   Psalm 31 (32) 1 Corinthians 10:31–11:1

WE CONTINUE TO READ from the opening chapter of the Gospel of Mark, and once again we are told about a healing worked by Jesus. This time it is the healing of a leper. In his desperation the leper violates the rules about keeping away from people. The reaction of Jesus mirrors the compassion of God. When our text says that Jesus was 'moved with pity' this points to the deep compassion of the loving God.

What is perhaps most remarkable about this miracle is that 'Jesus stretched out his hand and touched him'. Our first reading from the Book of Leviticus tells how lepers used to be taken to a priest and formally declared to be 'unclean'. They were banished and had to live apart. This was still the practice in Jesus' day.

Jesus' attitude is completely different. He is not afraid to violate the law by reaching out and touching the leper. In this way Jesus challenges the rules about what is 'clean', and what is 'unclean'.

In this miracle story it is by his touch and a simple word of command that Jesus heals the man. Perhaps surprisingly, Jesus then orders the healed man to comply with the law by going to a priest and making a thanksgiving offering for his recovery.

Jesus orders the man to tell nobody about his healing. This is a rather curious feature of the gospel, which shows that Jesus did not want popularity and was anxious that his work should not be misunderstood. But in his enthusiasm at being healed the man proclaims the word everywhere. The gospel ends with the irony that, while the leper rejoins society, Jesus the healer stays 'outside in deserted places'.

What does Jesus' acceptance of the leper teach us?

How do I try to reach out to those who are rejected by society?

Let us pray for a spirit of compassion and understanding.

Let us share the healed man's enthusiasm to make known the goodness of God.

Seventh Sunday in Ordinary Time (Year B)

Mark 2:1–12

When he returned to Capernaum, after some days word went round that he was in the house; and so many people collected that there was no room left, even in front of the door. He was proclaiming the word to them when some people came bringing him a paralytic carried by four men, but as they could not get the man to him through the crowd, they stripped the roof at the place where Jesus was; and when they had made an opening, they lowered the mat on which the paralytic lay. Seeing their faith, Jesus said to the paralytic, 'My child, your sins are forgiven.' Now some of the scribes were sitting there, and they discussed in their hearts, 'How can this man talk like that? It is blasphemy! Who can forgive sins but God alone?' And at once, Jesus, aware in his spirit that they were discussing like this, said to them, 'Why do you discuss these things in your hearts? Which is easier: to say to the paralytic, "Your sins are forgiven" or to say, "Get up, pick up your mat and walk"? But so that you may know that the Son of man has authority to forgive sins on earth' – he said to the paralytic – 'I say to you: get up, pick up your mat, and go off home.' And the man got up, and at once picked up his mat and walked out in front of everyone, so that they were all astonished and praised God saying, 'We have never seen anything like this.'

Other readings: Isaiah 43:18–19, 21–22, 24–25   Psalm 40 (41)
2 Corinthians 1:18–22

THE MIRACLE STORY WE read this Sunday presents several interesting aspects. First of all, it is a testimony to the faith of the four men who are determined despite all the obstacles to bring the paralytic to Jesus for healing. Earlier the disciples had taken Jesus to cure the mother-in-law of Simon. Now it is these men who facilitate the healing of their friend.

A second important aspect of the story is that Jesus begins by announcing the forgiveness of sins. He seems to be telling us that the inner healing of forgiveness is more important than physical well-being. It is possible to experience a deep inner peace, the peace of God, even in the midst of serious illness.

This story also includes a controversy. The paralytic says nothing in reply to Jesus' words of forgiveness, but the evangelist records the attitude of the scribes, experts in the Jewish law, who take offence at the words of Jesus. Jesus is aware of their thoughts and challenges them. For the first time Mark notes the antagonism between Jesus and the religious authorities. There will be frequent references to disputes and disagreements in the chapters which lie ahead. The reaction of the scribes in this passage stands in sharp contrast to the delight of the crowds, who praise God for the man's healing.

Am I eager to overcome any obstacles in the practice of my faith?
How much do I value the inner healing of forgiveness, and the
*   Sacrament of Reconciliation?*
Let us pray for a fuller understanding of the gifts brought by Christ.
Let us praise God for the healing and forgiveness which come to us
*   through Christ.*

Eighth Sunday in Ordinary Time (Year B)

Mark 2:18–22

John's disciples and the Pharisees were keeping a fast, when some people came to him and said to him, 'Why do John's disciples and the disciples of the Pharisees fast, but your disciples do not?' Jesus replied, 'Surely the bridegroom's attendants cannot fast while the bridegroom is with them? As long as they have the bridegroom with them, they cannot fast. But the days will come when the bridegroom is taken away from them, and then, on that day, they will fast. No one sews a piece of unshrunken cloth onto an old cloak; otherwise, the patch pulls away from it, the new from the old, and there is a worse tear. And nobody puts new wine into old wineskins; otherwise, the wine will burst the skins, and the wine is lost and the skins too. No! New wine into fresh skins!'

**Other readings: Hosea 2:16–17, 21–22   Psalm 102 (103)
2 Corinthians 3:1–6**

UP TO THIS POINT in the gospel of Mark we have heard about the call of the first disciples and the first healings of Jesus in and around Capernaum. Subsequently we hear of the first dispute of Jesus with those who disagree with him. This concerns the fact that Jesus eats and drinks with sinners and tax-collectors. He has come to call not the virtuous but sinners.

A further dispute ensues, this time about fasting, and Jesus introduces what might be considered his first parables. In the first, Jesus is the bridegroom whose friends rejoice at his presence. They surely cannot fast while he is with them. The image of the bridegroom reflects the first reading from Hosea, in which God is portrayed as the husband of his people Israel. The new bridegroom Jesus will one day be taken away from his friends, and then they will fast. The presence of the Messiah, however, brings a time of rejoicing and thanksgiving.

A further image concerns the repair of an old cloak. A new patch will not sit comfortably with the old since its strength will further undermine the weakness of the old. An entirely new cloak is required. The newness of the gospel is proclaimed. Similarly the new wine of the gospel requires new skins, for it is precious and must not be lost by being placed in old skins.

*Do I rejoice at the presence of the bridegroom, and am I willing to put
    on the new cloak of the gospel?*
*Am I willing to embrace what is new and different, and move on to
    the surprises of God?*
*Let us pray for a fuller understanding of how Jesus invites us to
    embrace what is new.*

Let us be willing to consider carefully the message of the gospel and its implications for our attitudes and actions.

Ninth Sunday in Ordinary Time (Year B)

Mark 2:23 – 3:6

It happened that one Sabbath he was taking a walk through the cornfields, and his disciples began to make a path by plucking ears of corn. And the Pharisees said to him, 'Look, why are they doing something on the Sabbath that is not permitted?' And he said to them, 'Have you never read what David did in his time of need when both he and his companions were hungry – how he went into the house of God when Abiathar was high priest, and ate the loaves of the offering which only the priests are permitted to eat, and how he also gave some to the men with him?' And he said to them, 'The Sabbath was made for man, not man for the Sabbath; so the Son of man is lord even of the Sabbath.'

Again he went into the synagogue, and there was a man present who had a withered hand. And they were watching him to see if he would cure him on the Sabbath day, so that they might accuse him. He said to the man who had the withered hand, 'Get up into the middle!' Then he said to them, 'Is it permitted on the Sabbath to do good, or to do evil; to save life, or to kill?' But they kept silence. Then he looked angrily round at them, grieved at their hardness of heart, and said to the man, 'Stretch out your hand.' He stretched it out and his hand was restored. The Pharisees went out and began at once to conspire with the Herodians against him, how to destroy him.

Other readings: Deuteronomy 5:12–15   Psalm 80 (81)
2 Corinthians 4:6–11

FURTHER CONTROVERSIES ARISE IN the early ministry of Jesus, one concerning the actions of the disciples and the other the action of Jesus. They focus on sabbath observance.

A strict interpretation of the law finds fault with the disciples, who due to hunger pick ears of corn on the Sabbath. Our first reading from Deuteronomy points out that observance of the Sabbath is the practice of a free people, who were once in slavery in Egypt. Excessive application of the same law enslaves rather than freeing. Jesus points to an episode in the story of David, in which the laws of the sanctuary were violated. Jesus rightly affirms that sabbath observance should benefit human beings. It is not a law to be fulfilled at all costs. Jesus is master of the Sabbath.

A sabbath action of Jesus, in healing the man with the withered hand, has another group take a stand against Jesus. They do not speak at all during the episode, but Jesus knows their thoughts and challenges their obsession with extreme sabbath observance. Jesus invites a fresh interpretation of the law, which, just as it viewed with mercy the hunger of the disciples, now makes allowance for the plight of the man with the withered hand. It is instructive that the first reference in Mark to plots to kill Jesus comes at this point.

Am I able, like Jesus, to temper strictness with mercy, and so to look at people's real needs?

How far am I willing to risk rejection and persecution for acting with compassion?

Let us ask ourselves about the appropriate observance of the Lord's day.

Let us be willing to review cherished practices to see whether they correspond to the mercy of Jesus.

Tenth Sunday in Ordinary Time (Year B)

Mark 3:20–35

He went home, and again such a crowd collected that they could not even have a meal. When his relations heard of this, they set out to take charge of him; for they said, 'He is out of his mind.'

The scribes who had come down from Jerusalem were saying, 'He has Beelzebul,' and, 'It is through the prince of demons that he drives demons out.' So he called them to him and spoke to them in parables, 'How can Satan drive out

Satan? If a kingdom is divided against itself, that kingdom cannot stand. And if a household is divided against itself, that household will not be able to stand. Now if Satan has risen up against himself and is divided, he cannot stand either – it is the end of him. But no one can make his way into a strong man's house and plunder his property unless he has first tied up the strong man. Only then will he plunder the house.

'Amen I say to you, everything will be forgiven to the children of men, all their sins and whatever blasphemies they make; but anyone who blasphemes against the Holy Spirit will never receive forgiveness, but is guilty of an eternal sin.' This was because they were saying, 'He has an unclean spirit.'

Now his mother and his brothers arrived and, standing outside, sent in a message calling him. And around him was sitting a crowd and they said to him, 'Look, your mother and brothers and sisters are outside asking for you.' He replied, 'Who are my mother and brothers?' And looking at those sitting in a circle round him, he said, 'Here are my mother and my brothers. Whoever does the will of God, that person is my brother and sister and mother.'

Other readings: Genesis 3:9–15 Psalm 129 (130) 2 Corinthians 4:13–5:1

IN THIS RATHER COMPLICATED gospel passage we hear about the reaction to Jesus' activity, from his family and from the religious authorities, represented by the scribes.

Members of his family are so concerned about Jesus that they consider taking him home by force to put an end to his ministry. But it is the scribes from Jerusalem who have worked out in their own way that Jesus is in league with the powers of evil, with Beelzebul, another name for Satan. Jesus takes this point up. His actions are constantly challenging the power of evil, so how can he be on the side of evil? He is in fact the one who is strong enough to challenge Satan. The scribes have closed their minds to this possibility; they are unwilling to let the Spirit teach them.

The final verses suggest that the relationships we make in the Christian family are of great significance.

Is the gospel of Jesus challenging to me?
Am I open enough to receive the message which Jesus brings?
Let us pray for those who struggle with the Christian gospel.
Let us pray for those who are stuck in their own dogmatism.

Eleventh Sunday in Ordinary Time (Year B)

Mark 4:26–34

He also said, 'This is what the kingdom of God is like. It is as if a man should scatter seed on the earth. Night and day, while he sleeps, when he is awake, the seed sprouts and grows; how, he does not know. Of its own accord the earth produces first the shoot, then the ear, then the full grain in the ear. And when the crop is ripe, at once he puts in the sickle, because harvest time has come.'

He also said, 'With what can we compare the kingdom of God? What parable can we find for it? It is like a mustard seed which, at the time of its sowing on the earth, is the smallest of all the seeds on earth. Yet once it is sown it grows up and becomes the biggest shrub of all and puts out big branches so that the birds of the air nest in its shade.'

Using many parables like these, he spoke the word to them, so far as they were capable of understanding it. He did not speak to them except in parables, but he explained everything to his disciples on their own.

Other readings: Ezekiel 17:22–24   Psalm 91 (92)   2 Corinthians 5:6–10

THE EVANGELIST MARK GATHERS together several of the parables of Jesus in what becomes chapter 4 of his gospel. Three of these parables speak of the growth of a seed. The parable of the sower, which comes at the start of the chapter, considered different responses to the preaching of the word of God. The parables before us now are concerned with other aspects of growth.

The first of our parables, known as the parable of 'the seed growing secretly' is unique to Mark, found in no other gospel. Its meaning is clear. Jesus is saying that the work of the kingdom of God is mysterious and profound. We do not understand how God works in the world, and within the human heart. But the work of God will achieve its purpose. The harvest will come, provided we do not thwart it. Our second parable, the parable of the mustard seed, shows another dimension. The mustard seed is tiny, but the growth of the kingdom is great. The kingdom, like the mustard shrub, provides shelter and shade. The kingdom of God provides support and sustenance.

Mark ends this section of parables by speaking of Jesus' purpose in using parables. His intention was not to confuse but to explain the work of God in the world and in the human heart. Those who are open to understanding will gradually come to know more. The work of the grace of Christ is slow but deep.

Why did Jesus use parables?
Which parables of Jesus are most memorable for you?
Pray for a deeper understanding of the message of Jesus.
Pray for the patience to let the grace of Jesus work in your heart.

Twelfth Sunday in Ordinary Time (Year B)

Mark 4:35–41

On that day, when it was getting late, he said to them, 'Let us cross over to the other side.' And leaving the crowd behind they took him, just as he was, in the boat; and there were other boats with him. Then a great squall of wind occurred and the waves were breaking into the boat so that it was already being swamped. But he was in the stern, asleep on the cushion. They woke him and said to him, 'Teacher, do you not care that we are lost?' And waking up he rebuked the wind and said to the sea, 'Quiet now! Be silent!' And the wind dropped, and there was a dead calm. Then he said to them, 'Why are you so cowardly? Have you still no faith?' They were overcome

with awe and said to one another, 'Who then is this, that
even the wind and the sea obey him?'

Other readings: Job 3:1, 8–11 Psalm 106 (107) 2 Corinthians 5:14–17

THE EARLY CHAPTERS OF the Gospel of Mark record Jesus'
activity in Galilee, as he preaches the good news of the kingdom
of God and performs mighty works which point to the approach
of the kingdom. All this precedes his journey to Jerusalem, and his
ministry there which leads to his death and resurrection. The mighty
work, or miracle, about which we hear in today's gospel reading, is
the calming of a storm on the Sea of Galilee.

Most of the miracles of Jesus are healings. The first healing in
Mark's gospel was that of the possessed man in the synagogue at
Capernaum. The evangelist also gives summaries of various healings
worked by Jesus. Along with the parables, the miracles are a major
feature of Jesus' ministry in Mark's gospel. This miracle shows the
power of Jesus over natural forces, as his words calm the sea and the
winds.

All four gospels recall such an event. The disciples call out to
Jesus in alarm, while he is asleep in the stern. His powerful word
recalls the word spoken by God in creation at the beginning of the
Book of Genesis. Our first reading from the Book of Job gives a
poetic description of God's power in limiting the extent of the seas.

The effect of the words of Jesus is instant. He has the power of
God. Jesus questions the disciples about their fear and their lack of
faith, but the passage ends with their question about Jesus. 'Who
can this be? Even the wind and the sea obey him.' The awe they
experience – the Greek text says 'they feared with a great fear' - is
the reaction of someone in the presence of God. The disciples will
be searching for an answer to their question throughout the gospel.

What is the meaning of the miracles of Jesus?
Does it seem strange to you that Jesus should put on such a
    display of power to calm the storm?
Pray for a deeper awareness of the purpose of Jesus and the
    gospel.
Pray for those who struggle to accept the truth about Jesus.

Thirteenth Sunday in Ordinary Time (Year B)

Mark 5:21–43

When Jesus had crossed again in the boat to the other side, a large crowd gathered round him and he stayed by the lake. Then one of the leaders of the synagogue named Jairus came up, and seeing him, fell at his feet and pleaded with him repeatedly, saying, 'My little daughter is at the point of death. Come and lay your hands on her that she may be saved and may live.' Jesus went with him and a large crowd followed him; they were jostling him.

Now there was a woman who had suffered from a haemorrhage for twelve years; having endured much under many physicians, she had spent all she had without getting any benefit from it; in fact, she was getting worse. She had heard about Jesus, and she came up through the crowd and touched his tunic from behind, thinking, 'If I can just touch his clothes, I shall be saved.' And at once the source of the bleeding dried up, and she felt in her body that she was cured of her sickness. And at once aware of the power that had gone out from him, Jesus turned round in the crowd and said, 'Who touched my clothes?' His disciples said to him, 'You see how the crowd is jostling you; how can you say, "Who touched me?"' But he began looking round to see who had done it. Then the woman came forward, in fear and trembling because she knew what had happened to her, and she fell before him and told him the whole truth. And he said to her, 'My daughter, your faith has saved you; go in peace and be free of your sickness.'

While he was still speaking some people arrived from the house of the leader of the synagogue to say, 'Your daughter is dead; why put the teacher to any further trouble?' But Jesus overheard what they were saying and he said to the leader of the synagogue, 'Do not be afraid; only have faith.' And he allowed no one to follow with him except Peter and James and John the brother of James. So they came to the house of the leader of the synagogue, and Jesus saw a commotion with people weeping and wailing unrestrainedly. He went in and said to them, 'Why all this commotion and crying? The child has not died, she is asleep.' But they ridiculed him. So he turned them all out and, taking with him the child's father and mother and his own companions, he went into the place where the child lay. And taking the child by the hand he said to her, '*Talitha kum!*' which means, 'Little girl, I say to you, get up.' And at once the little girl got up and began to walk around, for she was twelve years old. At once they were overcome with astonishment, and he gave them strict orders that no one should know about it, and said that she should be given something to eat.

**Other readings: Wisdom 1:13–15, 2:23–24   Psalm 29 (30)
2 Corinthians 8:7, 9, 13–15**

THIS IS A VERY LONG gospel reading in the lectionary. It includes both the raising of a little girl and the healing of an elderly woman. This is the only account in the Gospel of Mark of the raising of a person from the dead. We might recall the detailed story of the raising of Lazarus in John chapter 11. Both these accounts invite us to reflect on the gift of eternal life promised us by Jesus.

The theme of life after death is introduced in the first reading for today's Mass, from the Book of Wisdom. The writer explains that death was 'not God's doing', but is a consequence of 'the devil's envy'. Human beings are not made for death but for eternal life with God. This is demonstrated definitively in the resurrection of Jesus.

The evangelist records the Aramaic words *Talitha kum* used by Jesus on this occasion. When these words are translated into the Greek of the gospel the expression 'get up' employs a word commonly associated in the New Testament with the resurrection of Jesus. Another Greek word used of the resurrection occurs when the evangelist reports that the little girl 'got up'. The mighty works of Jesus are not simply meant to provoke astonishment and wonder among the witnesses. They also point Christian listeners to belief in the resurrection.

*How do the miracles of Jesus relate to the fundamental gospel message?
What in particular strikes you about the raising of Jairus' daughter?
Pray for a deeper understanding of the gospel.
Pray for those who are fearful of sickness and death.*

Fourteenth Sunday in Ordinary Time (Year B)

Mark 6:1-6

Leaving that district, he went to his home town, and his disciples followed him. With the coming of the Sabbath he began teaching in the synagogue, and many were astonished when they heard him. They said, 'Where did the man get all this? What is this wisdom that has been given to him, and such works of power as are worked by his hands? Is not this the carpenter, the son of Mary, the brother of James and Joset and Jude and Simon? And are not his sisters here with us?' And they took offence at him. And Jesus said to them, 'A prophet is without honour only in his own country, among his own kinsfolk and in his own house;' and he could do no work of power there, except that he cured a few sick people by laying his hands on them. He was amazed at their lack of faith.

Other readings: Ezekiel 2:2-5   Psalm 122 (123)   2 Corinthians 12:7-10

This gospel reading gives us an account of the visit of Jesus to his 'home town', which we know to be Nazareth. Just as he has already done in Capernaum, here too he teaches in the synagogue on the Sabbath. But the reaction of the townspeople is not positive. How can this local man be gifted with so many fine qualities? They are determined to find fault with his wisdom and with his actions.

They go on to speak of his family. They know his mother, and they know his relations. His humble origins rule out anything special. 'And they took offence at him.' The sense of the Greek word used here suggests they were determined to find excuses for not accepting him. John's gospel will express this with the momentous words: 'He came to his own, and his own would not accept him.' (John 1:11)

This passage is important in the unfolding drama of the gospel. It was not only the religious and political leaders who were against Jesus. Jesus quotes what seems to be a common proverb in antiquity: 'A prophet is only despised in his own home.' The passage ends with the strange remark that 'he could do no work of power there.' The healing work of Jesus is not forced on those who do not wish to receive it, and who are not open to the new deeds the Lord is doing.

The text from the prophet Ezekiel confirms that, like Jesus, the ancient prophets of Israel often experienced rejection. St Paul, facing 'a thorn in the flesh', hears those comforting words of the Lord: 'My grace is enough for you.' We too should trust the goodness of God in our efforts to witness to Christ.

What does the rejection of Jesus in Nazareth teach us?
What do you think motivated the attitude of Jesus' compatriots?
Let us pray for those who face opposition because they live according to the values of the gospel.
Let us pray for missionaries and for those who witness to the truth amid injustice.

Fifteenth Sunday in Ordinary Time (Year B)

Mark 6:7–13

Then he summoned the Twelve and began to send them out in pairs, giving them authority over the unclean spirits. And he instructed them to take nothing for the journey except a staff – no bread, no bag, no coppers for their belts. They were to wear sandals but not to put on two tunics. And he said to them, 'If you enter a house anywhere, remain there until you leave the place. And if any place will not welcome you and they do not listen to you, as you walk away shake off the dust from under your feet as evidence to them.' So they set off to proclaim conversion; and they kept casting out many demons, anointing many sick people with oil and curing them.

Other readings: Amos 7:12–15 Psalm 84 (85) Ephesians 1:3–14

EARLIER IN THE GOSPEL, in chapter 3, the evangelist told us of the choice of the Twelve by Jesus. They were to be his companions and to be sent out to preach and cast out devils. It comes as no surprise now that Jesus sends them out in twos 'with authority over unclean spirits'. Just as Jesus announces the coming of the Kingdom of God by preaching and mighty works, so too will the disciples confirm their preaching by their healing ministry.

They are to take no provisions for the journey. They are allowed a staff and sandals, which might have been considered essential for travelling on foot on the rough paths of rural Galilee, but they are not allowed to take provisions of any kind. They must trust that all will be provided. Furthermore, they are to remain at the house of whoever shows them hospitality.

Jesus has already spoken of the rejection of his preaching, the seed not growing to fruition. He has experienced the antagonism of the people of his own home town of Nazareth. He warns here of the lack of welcome the Twelve may experience. Some will be unwilling to listen to them. They are to shake the dust off their feet as they depart, showing that they cut all ties with those who refuse the good news.

The evangelist reports that the disciples, like Jesus, set off to 'proclaim conversion', and that they 'cast out demons', expelling the evil forces which were thought to cause suffering. We hear for the first time of the anointing of the sick with oil, and their healing. There are no reports in the gospels of Jesus using oil to anoint the sick.

In experiencing rejection both Jesus and the disciples follow in the footsteps of the prophets. Today we hear also of the banishment from Israel of the prophet Amos, who had sought to challenge the injustice practised in the kingdom.

Do you trust in the providence of God?
How can you offer others the good news of Jesus?
Let us pray for openness to the message of the gospel in our
*   society today.*
Let us pray for those who are anointed in the Sacrament of
*   the Sick.*

Sixteenth Sunday in Ordinary Time (Year B)

Mark 6:30–34

The apostles rejoined Jesus and reported to him all they had done and taught. And he said to them, 'Come away yourselves on your own to some lonely place and rest for a while'; for there were so many coming and going that they had no leisure even to eat. So they went off in the boat to a lonely place on their own. But people saw them going, and many recognised them; and from every town they all hurried to the place on foot and reached it before them. So as he stepped ashore he saw a large crowd; and he took pity on them because they were like sheep without a shepherd, and he began to teach them many things.

Other readings: Jeremiah 23:1–6 Psalm 22 (23) Ephesians 2:13–18

THE DISCIPLES HAVE BEEN sent out 'two by two' by Jesus in order to preach repentance and to heal the sick. After some time they return. While the evangelist normally refers to the followers of Jesus as 'disciples', those who are in the process of learning, as they return from their missions he calls them 'apostles', those sent out.

Jesus is concerned for their well-being and invites them to go with him to a lonely place in order to find peace and rest. It seems that the popularity of Jesus has influenced the mission of the disciples and that they too were in great demand. Their plan for some time of peace and quiet is frustrated. A crowd has already gathered at their destination. Mark speaks constantly in the early chapters of the gospel of the crowds who are eager for the words and works of Jesus.

This passage comes just before the multiplication of the loaves and fishes to feed the five thousand. Before giving them food to eat Jesus teaches them 'many things'. We see anticipated in this chapter the two ways in which Jesus continues to feed us: by Word and Sacrament. All this is motivated by his compassion for the crowd who are 'like sheep without a shepherd'.

The image of the shepherd who cares for the real needs of the sheep is often used in Scripture for those who have responsibility to care for people. The prophet Jeremiah speaks of the shepherds, in this case the rulers, who let the flock be destroyed and scattered, and looks forward to the coming of true shepherds. The psalm speaks of the Lord as the perfect shepherd who sees to the needs of his people, and the reading from Ephesians speaks of Christ as 'the peace between us', who reconciles Jew and Gentile.

Why is the image of the 'good shepherd' so popular?

How can we treasure more deeply the gifts of Word and Sacrament?

Let us pray for leaders who will have the good of their people as their priority.

Let us pray for those who are exhausted by ministering to others and can find no place of rest.

Seventeenth Sunday in Ordinary Time (Year B)

John 6:1–15

After this, Jesus crossed the Sea of Galilee – or of Tiberias – and a large crowd was following him, because they saw the signs he was doing for the sick. Jesus went up onto the mountain and sat down there with his disciples. The Passover, the festival of the Jews, was near. So Jesus, looking up and seeing that a large crowd was coming towards him, said to Philip, 'Where are we to buy bread so that these people may have something to eat?' He said this only to test him, for he himself knew what he was going to do. Philip answered him, 'Two hundred denarii worth of bread would not be enough for each of them to get a little.' One of his disciples, Andrew, Simon Peter's brother, said, 'There is a small boy here who has five barley loaves and two fish; but what is that among so many?' Jesus said, 'Make the people sit down.' There was plenty of grass in that place, so they sat down, as many as five thousand men. Then Jesus took the loaves, gave thanks, and distributed them to those who were sitting there, and the same with the fish, as much as they wanted. When they were satisfied he said to his disciples, 'Gather up the broken pieces left over, so that nothing is wasted.' So they gathered up the pieces and filled twelve large baskets with scraps left over from the five barley loaves by those who had eaten. Seeing the sign that he had done, the people were saying, 'This is indeed the prophet who is to come into the world.' Jesus, realising that they were about to come and take him by force and make him king, withdrew back to the mountain alone.

Other readings: 2 Kings 4:42–44 Psalm 144 (145) Ephesians 4:1–6

FOR THE NEXT FEW weeks our regular reading of the Gospel of Mark is interrupted as we read the sixth chapter of the Gospel of John. The chapter begins with the multiplication of the loaves, which is followed by extended words of Jesus in dialogue with the Jews.

The multiplication of the loaves and fishes, found in all the gospels, is in John's gospel one of the great signs. Seeing this 'sign' the people acclaim Jesus as a prophet, and there is a risk they will take him off to make him a king.

The miracle of Elisha narrated in the first reading serves to prepare for the greater sign worked by Jesus. The deeper sense of the sign will be explained by Jesus in the verses which follow.

Why is this miracle so important to all four evangelists?
How can we avoid misunderstanding the signs worked by Jesus?
Let us pray for true solidarity with those in need.
Let us pray for those who work that the hungry may be fed and that
*   unjust structures may be challenged.*

Eighteenth Sunday in Ordinary Time (Year B)

John 6:24–35

When the crowd saw that neither Jesus nor his disciples were there, they got into those boats themselves and crossed to Capernaum to look for Jesus. Finding him on the other side of the sea, they said to him, 'Rabbi, when did you get here?' Jesus answered:

'Amen, Amen I say to you,
you are looking for me not because you saw the signs,
but because you ate your fill of the bread.
Do not work for food that corrupts,
but work for food that endures for eternal life,
which the Son of man will give you,
for on him God the Father has set his seal.'

Then they said to him, 'What should we do to perform the works of God?'

Jesus answered and said to them, 'This is the work of God, that you should believe in the one he has sent.' So they said to him, 'What sign will you do, that we may see and believe in you? What work will you do? Our fathers ate manna in the desert, as it is written, *Bread from heaven he gave them to eat.*'

Jesus said to them:

'Amen, Amen I say to you,
it was not Moses who gave you the bread from heaven,
it is my Father who gives you the true bread from heaven,
for the bread of God
is the bread which comes down from heaven
and gives life to the world.'

They said to him, 'Sir, give us this bread always.' Jesus answered them:

'I am the bread of life.
No one who comes to me will ever be hungry;
no one who believes in me will ever be thirsty.

**Other readings: Exodus 16:2–4, 12–15 Psalm 77 (78)
Ephesians 4:17, 20–24**

AFTER THE MULTIPLICATION OF the loaves by Jesus, once the crowds have caught up with him again, there is a dialogue concerning the sign Jesus has worked. The crowds have interpreted the sign in a materialistic way. They want to make Jesus their king so that they can be sure of their supply of bread. The sign has not been understood.

Jesus invites them to believe in the one God has sent, but they clamour for a new sign. They disparage Jesus' works by referring to the manna Moses gave in the desert. Once again, Jesus challenges their interpretation. It is God who is the source of all good gifts. The new gift God is giving, if they could accept it, is the gift of himself, the 'bread of life'. The conversation should not be about material survival, but about life in its fulness. The theme of the 'bread of life' will continue as the chapter unfolds.

To what extent do I misunderstand the signs Jesus gives me?
Do I understand what it means to 'work for God'?
We pray for an understanding that faith can resolve our human
*   concerns.*
We pray for a deeper love of Christ as the one who satisfies our deepest
*   needs.*

Nineteenth Sunday in Ordinary Time (Year B)

John 6:41–51

Now the Jews were murmuring about him, because he said, 'I am the bread that came down from heaven,' and they were saying, 'Surely this is Jesus, son of Joseph, whose father and mother we know. How can he now say, "I have come down from heaven"?'

Jesus said in reply to them, 'Stop murmuring among yourselves.

'No one can come to me unless drawn by the Father who
    sent me,
and I will raise up that person on the last day.
It is written in the prophets,
And they shall all be taught by God;
everyone who has listened to the Father
and learnt from him,
comes to me.
Not that anybody has seen the Father,

except him who is from God:
he has seen the Father.
Amen, Amen I say to you,
one who believes has eternal life.
I am the bread of life.
Your fathers ate manna in the desert
and they died;
but this is the bread which comes down from heaven,
so that a person may eat of it and not die.
I am the living bread which has come down from heaven.
Anyone who eats of this bread will live for ever;
and the bread that I shall give
is my flesh, for the life of the world.'

Other readings: 1 Kings 19:4–8 Psalm 33 (34) Ephesians 4:30–5:2

THE DISCUSSION BETWEEN JESUS and the Jews about the 'bread of life' continues. Once again his listeners are stuck with human ways of perception. They cannot accept that there is anything more to Jesus than the man who was brought up in Nazareth. What sense can they make of him 'coming down from heaven'?

Jesus challenges their quarrelling and seeks to move the discussion to a deeper level. The focus of these verses is on Jesus as the one who brings true teaching. To learn from Jesus is to be fed indeed. To learn from Jesus is to come to know the Father. The stress is once again on believing in the words of the Son. These words, even in this present life, bring eternal life. Unlike the manna in the desert, the bread Jesus offers is a pledge of eternal life.

In the final verse we have the first reference to the 'flesh' of Jesus: 'the bread that I shall give is my flesh, for the life of the world'. The emphasis in this and the following verses will be on the Eucharist.

We are reminded of the self-giving of Jesus at the Last Supper and at the cross. Jesus is the Bread of Life both in his words of life, and in the sacrament of his body and blood. The reaction of his hearers is predictably one of puzzlement, as the following verses will show.

Do I really value the teaching of Jesus as revealing the Father?
Do I treasure the coming of Jesus in Word and Sacrament at Mass?

*We pray that we may move beyond earthly perceptions to openness to
    the things of God.*
*We pray that the Bread of Life will truly nourish us as individuals and
    as community.*

Twentieth Sunday in Ordinary Time (Year B)

John 6:51–58

Jesus said, 'I am the living bread which has come down from
heaven.
Anyone who eats of this bread will live for ever;
and the bread that I shall give
is my flesh, for the life of the world.'

Then the Jews started arguing among themselves, 'How can
this man give us his flesh to eat?'

So Jesus said to them:

'Amen, Amen I say to you,
if you do not eat the flesh of the Son of man
and drink his blood,
you have no life in you.
Anyone who does eat my flesh
and drink my blood has eternal life,
and I shall raise up that person on the last day.
For my flesh is true food
and my blood is true drink.
Whoever eats my flesh and drinks my blood
dwells in me
and I dwell in that person.
As the living Father sent me
and I live through the Father,
so whoever eats me will also live through me.
This is the bread which came down from heaven;

not like the bread our ancestors ate
and died.
Anyone who eats this bread will live for ever.'

Other readings: Proverbs 9:1–6 Psalm 33 (34) Ephesians 5:15–20

WE CONTINUE READING FROM the sixth chapter of the gospel
of John, which interrupts our regular reading of Mark's gospel on the
ordinary Sundays of Year B. This is an opportunity to reflect on the
words of Jesus about the Bread of Life, and indeed about the mystery
of the Eucharist.

In today's passage the focus is on eating the flesh of Jesus. The
Eucharist has throughout the ages been a source of controversy and
misunderstanding. Many people have echoed the question of the
Jews in this passage 'How can this man give us his flesh to eat?'

In speaking of his flesh and blood which he gives to us Jesus is
employing a metaphor for his very self. Just as he gave himself in
bread and wine to the disciples as a sign of his coming gift of his life
on the Cross, so whenever we celebrate the Eucharist we receive the
real Jesus, his 'body, blood, soul and divinity', his full self, but in such
a way that the real gift is hidden beneath the physical appearances
of bread and wine.

Sharing in the Eucharist brings intimacy with Jesus. This
intimacy is the pledge of eternal life. The ultimate focus is on the
gift of life. As Jesus draws life from the Father, so we draw life from
Jesus in the Eucharist.

*Am I prepared to accept the mystery of the Eucharist and by frequent
reception to deepen my intimacy with the Lord?*

*Am I faithful to the commitment to attend Mass each Sunday and on
the major feasts?*

*We pray that we will allow the Sacraments to lead us further into the
things of God.*

*We pray that our communities may grow in love of the Eucharist and
reverent celebration of Christ's gifts of Word and Sacrament.*

Twenty-first Sunday in Ordinary Time (Year B)

John 6:60–69

After hearing it, many of his followers said, 'This is hard language. How could anyone accept it?' Knowing that his followers were murmuring about it, Jesus said to them, 'Does this offend you? What if you should see the Son of man ascending to where he was before?

'It is the spirit that gives life,
the flesh is no help.
The words I have spoken to you are spirit
and life.

'But there are some of you who do not believe.' For Jesus knew from the beginning who did not believe and who was to betray him. And he said, 'This is why I told you that no one could come to me except by the gift of the Father.' After this, many of his disciples fell back and no longer walked with him.

Then Jesus said to the Twelve, 'Do you want to go away too?' Simon Peter answered him, 'Lord, to whom shall we go? You have the words of eternal life, and we believe and we know that you are the Holy One of God.'

Other readings: Joshua 24:1–2, 15–18   Psalm 33 (34)   Ephesians 5:21–32

WITH THIS GOSPEL PASSAGE we come to the end of the sixth chapter of the Gospel of John, which we have been reading over the last several weeks. The followers of Jesus are said to be struggling with his teaching in the dialogue with the Jews which follows the working of the sign of the feeding of the five thousand. Jesus has spoken of himself as the 'bread of life'. Early in the chapter this referred to his life-giving teaching, but in the later verses Jesus began to speak of people eating his flesh and drinking his blood, in a clear allusion to the Eucharist. It seems to be this teaching about the Eucharist that is difficult for some of his followers to accept.

There is a contrast here between the followers of Jesus and the chosen Twelve. It is the Twelve who are then challenged by Jesus: 'Do you want to go away too?' One can understand the perplexity of the ordinary followers, but from those who have been with Jesus throughout the ministry greater insight and greater fidelity might be expected. The response of Peter comes in a firm commitment to Jesus: 'Lord, to whom shall we go? You have the words of eternal life.' This speech of Peter, his profession of faith in the name of the others, recalls the reading from the Book of Joshua, in which the people newly arrived in the promised land renew their covenant commitment to be the people of God: 'We too will serve the Lord, for he is our God.'

Do I appreciate that the words of Jesus are truly words of life?
What has this chapter of John's gospel taught me?
We thank God for the gift of his Son, who is our Bread of Life.
We pray for those who have never known the words of eternal life, nor
*   had the opportunity to commit themselves to the service of God.*

Twenty-second Sunday in Ordinary Time (Year B)

Mark 7:1–8, 14–15, 21–23

The Pharisees and some of the scribes who had come from Jerusalem gathered round him, and they noticed that some of his disciples were eating with unclean hands, that is, without washing them. For the Pharisees, and all the Jews, never eat without washing their arms as far as the elbow, observing the tradition of the elders; and on returning from the marketplace they never eat without first sprinkling themselves. There are also many other traditions which they observe, concerning the washing of cups and pots and bronze dishes. So the Pharisees and scribes asked him, 'Why do your disciples not live according to the tradition of the elders but eat their food with unclean hands?' He answered, 'How rightly Isaiah prophesied about you hypocrites, as it is written:

This people honours me with their lips,
while their hearts are far from me
They worship me in vain
teaching human commandments as precepts.

'You put aside the commandment of God to observe human tradition.'

He called the crowd to him again and said, 'Listen to me, all of you, and understand. Nothing that goes into a person from outside can make that person unclean; it is the things that come out of a person that make a person unclean.

For it is from within, from the human heart, that evil plans emerge: fornication, theft, murder, adultery, avarice, malice, deceit, indecency, envy, slander, pride, folly. All these evil things come from within and make a person unclean.'

Other readings: Deuteronomy 4:1–2, 6–8 Psalm 14 (15)
James 1:17–18, 21–22, 27

OUR GOSPEL PASSAGE CONTAINS an account of a dispute between Jesus and the religious leaders, some of whom had come from Jerusalem, seemingly to investigate his teaching. The first focus of the argument is on the meaning of 'tradition' and the importance that should be given to it. The evangelist explains how various religious practices had built up over time. The challenge of Jesus is that such human practices can sometimes obscure the deeper demands of faith.

Jesus goes on to speak of the importance of what lies in our hearts. From a clean heart goodness will come forth. External observances, which have their own importance, can sometimes distract us from the real work on our hearts and minds.

Do I value the good traditions which have been passed on to me, or do
I belittle them as 'not moving with the times'?
Am I determined to purify my inner motives and the things of the
heart, rather than cloak them in external camouflage?
We thank God for the gifts of the Scriptures, the teaching of the Church
and the living tradition of faith.
We pray for sound judgement and good discernment.

Twenty-third Sunday in Ordinary Time (Year B)

Mark 7:31–37

Returning from the territory of Tyre, he went by way of Sidon towards the Lake of Galilee, right through the Decapolis territory. And they brought him a deaf man who had difficulty speaking; and they asked him to lay his hand on him. He took him away from the crowd on his own, put his fingers into the man's ears and spat and touched his tongue. Then looking up to heaven he sighed; and he said to him, 'Ephphatha,' that is, 'Be opened.' And his ears were opened, and at once the impediment of his tongue was loosened and he spoke correctly. And Jesus ordered them to tell no one about it, but the more he ordered them, the more widely they proclaimed it. Their admiration was unbounded, and they said, 'Everything he does is good, he makes the deaf hear and the dumb speak.'

Other readings: Isaiah 35:4–7   Psalm 145 (146)   James 2:1–5

THIS PARTICULAR MIRACLE STORY is only found in the Gospel of Mark. It happens in pagan territory, and is a sign of the openness of Jesus to healing all people. In this healing miracle Jesus uses different techniques to cure the man, including placing spittle on the man's tongue. Such techniques are known to have been used by other healers in ancient times, and it is remarkable that on occasion Jesus uses them too, perhaps to show that all healing is the work of God.

The word 'Ephphatha' is one of the rare instances of Aramaic words of Jesus being recorded by the evangelist. Aramaic was the native language of Jesus, while the gospels record everything in Greek, the international language of the day. The Aramaic word has to be written down in the gospel using Greek letters.

Hearing and speech are restored to the man, but Jesus then commands silence about the miracle. This is a particular feature of the gospel miracle stories and may be explained if we recall that Jesus was particularly concerned not to be made the leader of a popular movement, perhaps even a revolt against Roman rule. The purposes of the coming of Jesus are not involved with the politics of the day but with the true healing of people and societies.

The passage concludes with an allusion to the prophecy of Isaiah in our first reading. The days of the blind seeing, the deaf hearing and the dumb speaking were long desired by the people of former times. God's coming, it was hoped, would transform people's lives and the whole of creation. The miracle story suggests that these days have come. Who then is this man Jesus?

*How can I imitate Jesus' openness to people of different race and
    culture?*
What is my attitude to people with disabilities?
*Let us pray that we may use all our senses in the service of the gospel.
We pray for those who exercise healing ministries.*

Twenty-fourth Sunday in Ordinary Time (Year B)

Mark 8:27–35

Jesus and his disciples left for the villages round Caesarea Philippi. On the way he put a question to his disciples, saying to them, 'Who do people say I am?' And they told him, 'John the Baptist, others Elijah, others again, one of the prophets.' Then he himself put a further question to them, 'But you, who do you say I am?' In answer Peter said, 'You are the Messiah.' And he gave them strict orders not to tell anyone about him.

Then he began to teach them that the Son of man had to suffer much, and to be rejected by the elders and the chief priests and the scribes, and to be put to death, and after three days to rise again; and he said all this quite openly. Then, taking him aside, Peter began to rebuke him. But, turning and looking at his disciples, he rebuked Peter and said to him, 'Get behind me, Satan! You are thinking not as God thinks, but as humans do.'

He called together the crowd with his disciples and said to them, 'Anyone who wants to be a follower of mine must renounce self and take up the cross and follow me. For whoever wants to save life will lose it; but whoever loses life for my sake, and for the sake of the gospel, will save it.

Other readings: Isaiah 50:5–9 Psalm 114 (116) James 2:14–18

THE STORY TOLD IN this passage lies at the very heart of the drama of Mark's gospel. The question about the identity of Jesus is really a question about why he has come. People thought back to the great figures in the long history of the Jewish people as they attempted to understand the mission of Jesus. Jesus indeed shares the passion for the truth of John the Baptist, the strength and power of Elijah, and the spiritual qualities of other prophets. But Peter makes a greater claim for Jesus. He is the Messiah!

Jesus' reaction should be considered with care. He neither welcomes Peter's assertion nor rejects it. Jesus speaks for the first time of his suffering, death and resurrection. In doing so he challenges Peter's expectations about the Messiah, which were no doubt shared by others. The Messiah will not claim power for himself; he will not dominate others. On the contrary, others will have power over him; he will be dominated.

In giving up his life Jesus opens up a new way, a new vision, a vision of self-giving love. From this point onwards the Gospel of Mark will draw us inexorably into the mystery of the cross, the mystery of God's love revealed in the human life of the Son of God, which explains the meaning and purpose of our own lives too.

Who is Jesus for me?
Am I willing to accept Jesus' words about the cross?
Let us pray for fidelity and courage as we discover more about God's
purposes.
Let us pray for all disciples of the Lord.

Twenty-fifth Sunday in Ordinary Time (Year B)

Mark 9:30–37

After leaving that place they made their way through Galilee; and he did not want anyone to know, for he was instructing his disciples; he was telling them, 'The Son of man is to be delivered into the power of men; they will put him to death; and when he has been put to death after three days he will rise again.' But they did not understand what he said and were afraid to ask him.

They came to Capernaum, and when he got into the house he asked them, 'What were you arguing about on the road?' They said nothing, because on the road they had been arguing with one another which of them was the greatest. So he sat down, called the Twelve to him and said, 'Anyone who wants to be first must be last of all and servant of all.' He then took a little child whom he set among them, and taking it in his arms he said to them, 'Whoever welcomes one little child such as this in my name, welcomes me; and whoever welcomes me, welcomes not me but the one who sent me.'

Other readings: Wisdom 2:12, 17–20 Psalm 53 (54) James 3:16–4:3

THE SECOND HALF OF the Gospel of Mark is dominated by the journey towards Jerusalem, the place of the death and resurrection of Jesus. Since this gospel is comparatively short, the tension of this journey is more evident than in the other gospels, as Jesus draws his reluctant and confused disciples to face the mystery of his cross.

For the second time Jesus announces his coming death. He will be handed over and put to death. Three days after he will rise again. While Peter had reacted strongly to similar words of Jesus in the previous chapter, here there is simply bewilderment.

The following verses underline that the disciples are not yet ready to face up to what Jesus has said. Their preoccupation is still with status and their relative positions in Jesus' company. Mark does not hesitate to present the disciples as having much to learn, both about the conditions for following Jesus and about the prospect of his martyrdom.

Jesus' answer is to call them to accept the position of the least, and he illustrates this by placing a child before them.

Our first reading, from the Book of Wisdom, speaks of the plots of the godless against the virtuous man. It is not surprising that Christians used such texts to reflect on what happened to Jesus. So should we.

How difficult is it to accept a crucified Messiah?

Do I, like the disciples, seek to avoid awkward truths which are
*   presented to me?*

We pray for those who face persecution and violence because of their
*   beliefs.*

We pray for the gift of true humility and appropriate ambition.

Twenty-sixth Sunday in Ordinary Time (Year B)

Mark 9:38–43, 45, 47–48

John said to him, 'Teacher, we saw someone who does not follow us driving out demons in your name, and because he does not follow us we tried to stop him.' But Jesus said, 'Do not stop him; no one who works a deed of power in my name could soon afterwards speak evil of me. Anyone who is not against us is for us.

'If anyone gives you a cup of water to drink because you bear the name of Christ, then, Amen I say to you, that person will most certainly not lose the reward.

'But anyone who causes one of these little ones who have faith to stumble, would be better thrown into the sea with a great millstone round the neck. And if your hand should cause you to stumble, cut it off; it is better for you to enter into life crippled, than to have two hands and go to hell, into the fire that can never be put out. And if your foot should cause you to stumble, cut it off; it is better for you to enter into life lame, than to have two feet and be thrown into hell. And if your eye should cause you to stumble, tear it out; it is better for you to enter into the kingdom of God with one eye, than to have two eyes and be thrown into hell where *their worm does not die and their fire is not extinguished.*'

Other readings: Numbers 11:25–29 Psalm 18 (19) James 5:1–6

THIS GOSPEL READING CONTAINS a collection of different sayings of Jesus. The first speech warns us against the exclusive attitude which says that, unless someone completely shares our opinions and our faith, they can do no good. The next saying seems to confirm this. Any good deed from whatever source, Jesus implies, should be welcomed and will be rewarded.

Jesus then speaks of 'obstacles' placed in the way of believers, the 'little ones' who have faith. The Greek word used here is similar to the word 'scandal'. To scandalise others, to violate their faith, to undermine their pursuit of what is good and right, is plainly wrong.

Jesus then apparently suggests that self-mutilation, cutting off hand or foot, and tearing out the eye, would be better than sinning. What are we to make of this? This is an extreme way of pointing out the seriousness of sin. Christians should understand the strength of what Jesus is saying, but Christian teaching has never condoned self-harm of this magnitude.

Finally, what are we to make of the references to hell and its eternal fire? The Church teaches us that the image of eternal fire is an attempt to express the dreadful pain of losing God and of shutting oneself off from the love of others. This pain is worse than any physical suffering.

How accepting am I of the goodness of those who do not share my beliefs?

Do I place obstacles in the way of others, undermining their faith and goodness?

We pray for the zeal which always seeks what is good.

We pray for confidence in the goodness of God.

Twenty-seventh Sunday in Ordinary Time (Year B)

Mark 10:2–16

Some Pharisees approached him and, to test him, asked, 'Is it permissible for a man to divorce his wife?' He answered them, 'What did Moses command you?' They replied, 'Moses commanded to draw up a writ of dismissal, and so divorce.'

Then Jesus said to them, 'It was in view of your hardness of heart that he wrote this commandment for you. But from the beginning of creation *he made them male and female. This is why a man will leave his father and mother, and the two become one flesh.* They are no longer two, therefore, but one flesh. So then, what God has united, no one may separate.' Back in the house the disciples questioned him about this, and he said to them, 'Whoever divorces his wife and marries another commits adultery against her. And if a woman divorces her husband and marries another she commits adultery.'

People were bringing little children to him, for him to touch them. The disciples rebuked them, but when Jesus saw this he was indignant and said to them, 'Let the little children come to me; do not stop them; for it is to such as these that the kingdom of God belongs. Amen I say to you, whoever does not welcome the kingdom of God like a little child will never enter it.' Then he took them in his arms, and blessed them, laying his hands upon them.

Other readings: Genesis 2:18–24 Psalm 127 (128) Hebrews 2:9–11

JESUS, ON HIS JOURNEY to Jerusalem, has reached Judaea and some Pharisees question him about divorce. In answer Jesus quotes from the Book of Genesis some words which appear also at the end of our first reading: 'This is why a man will leave his father and mother, and the two become one flesh.' Jesus reasserts teaching about marriage which people in earlier times were unwilling to accept, because of their 'hardness of heart'. It calls for commitment and fidelity. The second piece of teaching is also relevant to families and relationships. The treatment of children is crucial to the health of a community.

Fidelity in marriage and a common endeavour to face difficulties are much needed in our time. The safety of children is an enormous concern and is rightly a priority. Not every marriage is ideal and there are some which cannot continue due to irreconcilable differences. In such situations great unhappiness can be experienced. Commitment and faithfulness, and loving guidance of young people and children, remain the basic foundations of a healthy and happy society. These are God-given principles, which reflect the faithful goodness of God.

How faithful am I to commitments undertaken?
Do I cherish those who are close to me?
We pray for our families that they may show courage and true love.
We pray for families who have suffered break-down that they may
*   receive strength and support to rebuild shattered lives.*

Twenty-eighth Sunday in Ordinary Time (Year B)

Mark 10:17–30

He was setting out on a journey when a man ran up, knelt before him and put this question to him, 'Good teacher, what must I do to inherit eternal life?' Jesus said to him, 'Why do you call me good? No one is good but God alone. You know the commandments: *You shall not murder; You shall not commit adultery; You shall not steal; You shall not give false witness; You shall not defraud; Honour your father and mother.'* And he said to him, 'Teacher, I have kept all these since my youth.' Jesus looked hard at him and loved him and said, 'You are lacking in one thing: go, sell whatever you own and give the money to the poor, and you will have treasure in heaven; then come, follow me.' But at this saying he baulked and he went away grieving, for he had many possessions.

Jesus looked round and said to his disciples, 'How hard it will be for those who have riches to enter the kingdom of God!' The disciples were astounded by these words, but Jesus again replied saying, 'My children, how hard it is to enter the kingdom of God! It is easier for a camel to pass through the eye of a needle than for someone rich to enter the kingdom of God.' They were more astonished, saying to one another, 'Then who can be saved?' Jesus gazed at them and said, 'By human resources it is impossible, but not for God: for to God everything is possible.'

Peter began saying to him, 'Look! We have left everything and followed you.' Jesus said, 'Amen I say to you, there is no one who has left house, brothers, sisters, mother, father, children or land for my sake and for the sake of the gospel who will not receive now in this present time a hundred times as much, houses, brothers, sisters, mothers, children and land – and persecutions too – and, in the age to come, eternal life.

Other readings: Wisdom 7:7–11   Psalm 89 (90)   Hebrews 4:12–13

AFTER THE INITIAL DISCUSSION about eternal life, Jesus addresses an issue which has always faced Christians. Are riches an obstacle to faith? Jesus' answer is that riches can be an impediment to the life of a disciple. The astonishment of the disciples arises from the belief that material prosperity is a reward from God. Jesus does not seem to share this view.

Instead, Jesus maintains that material possessions may well be an obstacle to salvation. For this reason Christians are invited 'to leave everything'. If this is not possible they should ensure that whatever they possess and whatever power they have is used for the good of others. The real enemy is selfishness. It is selfishness that kills love.

What is my attitude to my material possessions?
Do I allow selfishness to dominate my life, or any part of it?
Let us pray for those who have left everything in order to serve Christ.
Let us pray for wisdom and courage as we seek to live in a similar way.

Twenty-ninth Sunday in Ordinary Time (Year B)

Mark 10:35–45

James and John, the sons of Zebedee, approached him saying, 'Teacher, we want you to do for us whatever we ask you.' He said to them, 'What do you want me to do for you?' They said to him, 'Grant us to sit one at your right hand and the other at your left in your glory.' But Jesus said to them, 'You do not know what you are asking. Can you drink the cup that I drink, or be baptised with the baptism with which I am baptised?' They replied, 'We can.' Jesus said to them, 'The cup that I shall drink you shall drink, and with the baptism with which I shall be baptised you shall be baptised, but as for sitting at my right hand and my left, this is not mine to grant; this is for those for whom it has been prepared.'

When the other ten heard this they began to feel indignant with James and John, so Jesus called them to him and said to them, 'You know that among the gentiles those who are known as rulers lord it over them, and their great men tyrannise them. Among you this is not so, but whoever wants to become great among you must be your servant, and whoever wants to be first among you must be servant to all. For the Son of man came not to be served but to serve, and to give his life as a ransom for many.'

Other readings: Isaiah 53:10–11   Psalm 32 (33)   Hebrews 4:14–16

AS WE HAVE FOLLOWED the journey of Jesus to Jerusalem in previous gospel passages we have heard him speak repeatedly of what faces him there. Each time he tells the disciples of his coming death and resurrection, they are reluctant to face the painful reality. In this passage, once Jesus has spoken of his death for a third time, James and John demonstrate how disconnected they are from Jesus. They crave the best places in the kingdom.

Jesus' response focuses once again on the call to martyrdom. Are they willing to drink the cup and to be baptised in suffering? The two brothers say they are. Nevertheless, rewards in the kingdom are not assured. For Jesus such matters are for the Father.

The disciples need further teaching from Jesus. The ambitions of the disciple should not be those of the people of the world. They should not crave status and power, but the place of the slave, for they are the disciples of the one who came 'not to be served, but to serve' and to give his life as 'a ransom for many'. Jesus seems to be alluding here to the role of the servant as described in our first reading from the book of Isaiah. The servant offers his life in 'atonement' for the sins of many. 'By his wounds we have been healed.'

Do I share the ambition of James and John for the best seats in the
    kingdom?
Do I endeavour to unite the sufferings in my life with the suffering of
    Christ?
Let us thank God for the saving work of Christ the servant.
Let us be grateful for the witness of the martyrs of our own time.

Thirtieth Sunday in Ordinary Time (Year B)

Mark 10:46–52

They reached Jericho; and as he left Jericho with his disciples
and a great crowd, Bartimaeus – that is, the son of Timaeus
– a blind beggar, was sitting at the side of the road. When
he heard that it was Jesus of Nazareth, he began to cry out,
saying, 'Son of David, Jesus, have mercy on me.' And many
of them rebuked him and told him to keep quiet, but he
only cried out much more, 'Son of David, have mercy on
me.' Jesus stopped and said, 'Call him here.' So they called
the blind man saying, 'Courage! Get up, he is calling you.' So
throwing off his cloak, he jumped up and went to Jesus. Then
Jesus replied by saying, 'What do you want me to do for you?'
The blind man said to him, '*Rabbuni*, let me see again.' Jesus
said to him, 'Go, your faith has saved you.' And at once he
could see again and followed him along the road.

Other readings: Jeremiah 31:7–9 Psalm 125 (126) Hebrews 5:1–6

WITH THIS GOSPEL PASSAGE we reach the end of chapter 10 of
the Gospel of Mark, and, more significantly, we are reaching the end
of the journey of Jesus to Jerusalem. At the beginning of the next
chapter Mark will recount the triumphal entry of Jesus into the holy
city. During the journey Jesus has spoken on three clear occasions
of his coming suffering and death, and he has attempted to teach the
disciples about the mystery of martyrdom, the martyrdom which he
and they must face.

    What place does our present passage have in the story?

Bartimaeus reminds us of the basics as he sits 'by the road'. Human beings are in need of healing and forgiveness, and these are the things that Jesus provides. He calls out to Jesus with the title 'Son of David'. He has an inkling that he is the Messiah, but he will have had little idea that the Messiah is called to suffer and die in Jerusalem. Nevertheless, his call of faith is heard and Jesus in turn calls Bartimaeus to him. He is told to 'get up', an expression which would have reminded the early Christians of the resurrection. His rising up in faith and his subsequent healing point to the full gift of new life through faith in Jesus.

The gift of sight to Bartimaeus symbolises the gift of faith. Faith allows us to see with open eyes and a true heart. Unlike an earlier healing of a blind man in Mark, Jesus heals by word alone. The faith of Bartimaeus triggers the command of healing from Jesus. This time there is no delay in the healing. Bartimaeus receives his sight without delay. He becomes a disciple and follows Jesus along the road, exultant, on the last stages of the journey towards Jerusalem.

Do I seek true vision?
How determined am I to be healed by Jesus and to become his disciple?
Let us thank God for the light of faith.
Let us pray for all teachers of the faith that they may bring the light of truth to those to whom they minister.

Thirty-first Sunday in Ordinary Time (Year B)

Mark 12:28–34

One of the scribes who had heard them debating appreciated that Jesus had given them a good answer, and put a further question to him, 'Which is the first of all the commandments?' Jesus replied, 'This is the first: *Listen, Israel, the Lord our God is the one Lord, and you shall love the Lord your God with all your heart, and with all your soul, with all your mind and with all your strength.* The second is this: *You shall love your neighbour as yourself.* There is no commandment greater than these.' The scribe said to him, 'Well spoken, teacher;

what you have said is true, that *he is one and there is no other.* To *love him with all your heart, with all your understanding and strength*, and to *love your neighbour as yourself*, this is far more important than whole burnt offerings and sacrifices.' Jesus, seeing that he had answered wisely, said, 'You are not far from the kingdom of God.' And after that no one dared to question him any more.

Other readings: Deuteronomy 6:2–6 Psalm 17 (18) Hebrews 7:23–28

JESUS IS NOW in Jerusalem and the evangelist Mark gives us an account of his activities there. He has several encounters with the religious teachers. In this particular meeting there is no animosity. It is a peaceful dialogue between those who seek to do God's will.

The passage shows how Jesus' teaching takes the Hebrew Scriptures as its starting point. The words of Scripture Jesus speaks here are the same words we have already heard in the first reading from the Book of Deuteronomy, which includes in its final verses the Jewish prayer known commonly as the *Shema'* ('listen, Israel).

To these words taken from Deuteronomy Jesus adds a quotation from Leviticus, another book of the Law, which commands love of neighbour.

The conversation with the scribe continues by raising a point very frequently made by the prophets of the Old Testament and by Jesus: love of God and of neighbour is of more importance than 'burnt offerings and sacrifices'.

There is a profound agreement between Jesus and the teachers of Judaism. The tragedy which follows comes when worldly calculations are seen to be more important than seeking together to do the will of God. It is a situation repeated with dreadful regularity throughout the history of the world.

Do I seek to follow the great commandments given by God and restated by Jesus?

Do I cherish the Jewish foundations of my faith and seek to understand them?

Let us pray for the Jewish people, the first to hear the word of God.

Let us pray for all involved in peaceful dialogue between faiths.

Thirty-second Sunday in Ordinary Time (Year B)

Mark 12:38–44

In his teaching he said, 'Beware of the scribes who like to walk about in long robes, to be greeted respectfully in the market squares, to take the front seats in the synagogues and the places of honour at banquets. These are the men who devour the property of widows and, as an excuse, offer long prayers. The more severe will be the sentence they receive.'

He sat down opposite the treasury and watched the people putting money into the treasury, and many of the rich put in a great deal. A poor widow came and put in two small coins, of very little value. Then he called his disciples and said to them, 'Amen I say to you, this poor widow has put in most of all who are putting money into the treasury; for they have all put in money they could spare, but she out of her poverty has put in everything she possessed, all she had to live on.'

Other readings: 1 Kings 17:10–16 Psalm 145 (146) Hebrews 9:24–28

WE ARE APPROACHING THE end of our reading of the gospel of Mark. Today's reading provides a contrast: the self-assured scribes parading their virtue, and the humble widow offering all she had to live on.

Jesus attacks the hypocrisy of those religious people who make an outward show of virtue, but whose hearts are full of greed. His words against such behavior are harsh: they will receive a severe sentence. Such texts as this are sometimes used as a pretext for a general denigration of all the teachers of Judaism. We must bear in mind that the gospels also tell us of good and virtuous scribes and Pharisees.

Jesus observes the generosity of the poor widow. Unlike the scribes he has previously criticized, she does not trumpet her virtue. Almost unnoticed, she gives all she can for the upkeep of the temple of God. Jesus then 'called the disciples and said to them'. In this way the evangelist underlines this teaching of Jesus.

Our first reading, from the first Book of Kings, portrays another widow, the widow of Sidon who is suffering from a punishing famine.

Like the widow in the gospel, she shows remarkable generosity and trust in God. Though she does not have enough for herself and her son, she agrees to prepare something to eat for Elijah too, with remarkable consequences. Her example of faith is recalled by Jesus in chapter 4 of Luke's gospel.

Do I parade my good deeds before others in order to appear better than I am?

Am I prepared to take risks in being generous?

Let us pray for a spirit of thankfulness and generous sharing of what we have.

Let us pray that those who are immersed in selfishness will take up the call to share with the poor.

Thirty-third Sunday in Ordinary Time (Year B)

Mark 13:24–32

Jesus said, 'But in those days, after that distress, *the sun will be darkened, the moon will not give its light, the stars will be falling* out of the sky and the powers in the heavens will be shaken. And then they will see the *Son of man coming in clouds* with great power and glory. And then he will send the angels and gather his elect from the four winds, from the ends of the world to the ends of heaven.

'From the fig tree learn a parable: as soon as its twigs grow supple and it puts out leaves, you know that summer is near. So with you when you see these things happening: know that it is near, at the gates. Amen I say to you, this generation will not pass away before all these things take place. Heaven and earth will pass away, but my words will not pass away. But as for that day or hour, nobody knows it, neither the angels in heaven, nor the Son; no one but the Father.'

Other readings: Daniel 12:1–3 Psalm 15 (16) Hebrews 10:11–14, 18

OUR GOSPEL READING TODAY is taken from the final chapter of the story of the ministry of Jesus in the Gospel of Mark. In chapter 14 the story of the Passion will begin. In this chapter, Jesus looks to the future and talks about the things that are to come and about the end of time. He has encouraged his disciples to face wars, disasters and persecutions. There will be a 'time of distress' to be endured by all.

Jesus' words become much more dramatic as he talks about cosmic events. He uses the language customary at the time to speak of the end of the world. The climax will be the coming of 'the Son of Man'. Jesus takes this concept from the Book of Daniel and applies it to himself. At his glorious return his followers will be gathered together from all corners of the earth.

People have questioned and speculated about the end of the world, and in particular about the time of its happening. Having spoken of the signs that will precede it, Jesus gives a warning: no-one but the Father knows the time of the end. It is useless to speculate about all this, but, as the gospels repeatedly urge us, we are to live in readiness for the end of our lives. The final message of Jesus' teaching in Mark's gospel is that we should 'Stay awake!' We are called to live in imitation of the Son of Man, who came to serve and to give his life as a ransom for us.

Do I look forward to the gathering together of all God's people?

What have I learnt from the liturgical reading of the Gospel of Mark this year?

Let us pray for trustfulness and courage as we face life's trials.

Let us pray for serenity and confidence in the loving kindness of God, whose plans for the world will come to completion in a way and at a time we do not know.

Christ the King (Year B)

John 18:33–37

So Pilate went back into the Praetorium and called Jesus to him and asked him, 'Are you the king of the Jews?' Jesus replied, 'Do you ask this on your own account, or have others spoken to you about me?' Pilate answered, 'Am I a Jew? Your own people and the chief priests handed you over to me: what have you done?' Jesus replied, 'My kingdom is not of this world; if my kingdom were of this world, my officers would have fought to prevent me being surrendered to the Jews. As it is, my kingdom is not from here.' Pilate said, 'So, then you are a king?' Jesus answered, 'You say that I am a king. I was born for this, I came into the world for this, to bear witness to the truth; and everyone who belongs to the truth listens to my voice.'

Other readings: Daniel 7:13–14   Psalm 92 (93)   Apocalypse 1:5–8

THE FINAL SUNDAY IN our liturgical year is the feast of Christ the King. The theme of the kingship of Christ should not be misunderstood. Jesus is not king in an earthly sense. The acclamations of the crowds on Palm Sunday and the enthusiastic endorsement of the disciples that Jesus is the Messiah might mislead us. Jesus is king, Jesus is Messiah, because he is the anointed one of God, who comes to do the will of God. For the evangelist John, Christ's kingship is revealed above all on the cross.

In the dialogue with Pilate in the Fourth Gospel Jesus points Pilate in the right direction: his kingdom is not an earthly one. He came 'to bear witness to the truth'. Those who seek the truth are members of his kingdom, which our liturgy today describes in the Preface as 'a kingdom of truth and life, a kingdom of holiness and grace, a kingdom of justice, love and peace'. Pilate's dismissive answer to Jesus will be 'Truth, what is that?'

Reading the gospels throughout the liturgical year we are presented with a choice, whether, like Pilate, to pursue earthly values or, alternatively, to pursue the truth. In each of the four gospels Jesus bears witness above all to the truth that God is a God of love to be loved without reserve. We see that above all in his triumph on the cross.

Our second reading today from the Book of the Apocalypse speaks of Jesus as one 'who loves us and has washed away our sins with his blood'. His death brings us forgiveness and is our liberation. He is king because he leads us to the fulness of life and to the truth. He has made us 'a line of kings, priests to serve his God and Father'. The vocation of each one of us is to lead others to the truth we have come to know through Jesus and to make of our lives a gift of service to our loving God.

In what sense is Jesus a king?

Do I realise that at Baptism I became a member of the kingly and priestly people of Christ?

Let us pray that we may always be faithful to the truth we have learnt from Christ.

We pray that, with our brothers and sisters who have gone before us in faith, we may come to share in God's kingdom of truth and love.

Sundays
in
Ordinary
Time

YEAR C

Second Sunday in Ordinary Time (Year C)

John 2:1–11

On the third day there was a wedding at Cana in Galilee, and the mother of Jesus was there, Jesus and his disciples had also been invited to the wedding. When the wine ran out, the mother of Jesus said to him, 'They have no wine.' Jesus said to her, 'Woman, what is that to me and to you? My hour has not yet come.' His mother said to the servants, '*Do whatever he tells you*'. There were six stone water jars there, in accordance with the purification rites of the Jews: each could hold about a hundred litres. Jesus said to them, 'Fill the jars with water,' and they filled them to the brim. Then he said to them, 'Now draw some out and take it to the president of the feast.' They took it. When the president tasted the water that had become wine, and did not know where it came from – though the servants who had drawn the water knew – he called the bridegroom and said, 'Everyone serves good wine first and the less good wine when the guests have drunk deep; but you have kept the best wine till now.'

Jesus did this, the first of his signs, at Cana of Galilee. He revealed his glory, and his disciples believed in him.

Other readings: Isaiah 62:1–5 Psalm 95 (96) 1 Corinthians 12:4–11

THIS SUNDAY'S GOSPEL SHOWS our reluctance to leave the Christmas season behind. It tells of the third of the 'manifestations' of Jesus associated with the Christmas season, the others being the Epiphany and the Baptism of the Lord. The key to understanding the place of today's gospel in our liturgy is the statement that 'He let his glory be seen.' The Gospel of John contains seven major signs by which the true identity of Jesus, his glory, is made known.

The transformation of the water into wine tells us that Jesus brings a new time, a time of richness and fulfilment. An enormous amount of wine is provided. Although the 'hour' of Jesus, the hour of his death and resurrection, has not yet come, this sign is a pointer towards the 'glory' of Jesus.

The role of the mother of Jesus, who is addressed by Jesus as 'Woman', is significant. As in the stories of Jesus' birth, so here in John, she collaborates with God's ways in a humble and self-giving manner. She is the woman of the new covenant, as Eve was the woman of the old.

What is the role of the mother of Jesus in the events of our salvation?
What do I take away from the Christmas season as ordinary time takes over?
Pray for the vision to see the hidden glory of God in today's world.
Pray for those who are searching for the signs of God's presence.

Third Sunday in Ordinary Time (Year C)

Luke 1:1–4 4:14–21

Since many others have undertaken to draw up an account of the events that have reached their fulfilment among us, as they were handed down to us by those who from the beginning were eyewitnesses and servants of the word, I too, after carefully going over everything from the beginning, have decided to write an ordered account for you, most excellent Theophilus, so that you may know for certain the truth about the teaching that you have received.

Jesus returned to Galilee in the power of the Spirit, and his reputation spread throughout the countryside. He kept teaching in their synagogues and was glorified by everyone.

He came to Nazara, where he had been brought up, and went into the synagogue on the Sabbath as was his custom. He stood up to read, and he was given the scroll of the prophet Isaiah. Unrolling the scroll he found the place where it is written:

The spirit of the Lord is upon me,
for he has anointed me to bring good news to the poor.

He has sent me to proclaim release to captives,
sight to the blind, to let the oppressed go free,
to proclaim a year of the Lord's favour.

He then rolled up the scroll, gave it back to the assistant and sat down. And the eyes of all in the synagogue were fixed on him. Then he began to speak to them, 'Today this text has been fulfilled in your hearing.'

Other readings: Nehemiah 8:2–6, 8–10   Psalm 18 (19)
1 Corinthians 12:12–30

THIS SUNDAY WE FINALLY begin our reading of the Gospel of Luke, the gospel laid down to be read in Year C. There are two separate passages in today's gospel reading. We begin with the opening four verses of chapter 1, in which the evangelist sets down his method of working and his intention. Luke tells us that others evangelists have already written gospels. His sources are eye-witnesses of Jesus, and those who have preached the gospel. Luke assures Theophilus, to whom the gospel is addressed, and all who hear or read it, that the gospel is trustworthy.

Luke begins the story of Jesus' ministry with his visit to the synagogue in Nazareth. Jesus reads from the book of Isaiah at the sabbath service, and declares that the text he reads is being fulfilled. Luke wants us to recognize that Jesus is the long-awaited anointed one of God (the Messiah, the Christ). He brings 'good news to the poor', not those who have little in a worldly sense, but those who recognize their poverty in the sight of God, their need of God. Luke is already answering the question 'Who is Jesus?' The Nazareth story will continue next week.

What can we deduce from this gospel about how the gospels came to
   be written?
What do you understand by the word 'fulfilment'?
Let us pray that our hearts will be open to new insights as we begin
   reading Luke and celebrate the Sunday of the Word of God.
Let us pray that we ourselves may be 'good news to the poor'.

Fourth Sunday in Ordinary Time (Year C)

Luke 4:21–30

Then he began to speak to them, 'Today this text has been fulfilled in your hearing.' And all bore witness to him, and were astonished by the words of grace that came from his lips.

They said, 'Is not this the son of Joseph?' But he replied, 'No doubt you will quote me the saying, "Physician, heal yourself. Do here also in your own country what we have heard has been happening in Capernaum."' And he said, 'Amen I say to you, no prophet is ever accepted in his own country. In truth I tell you, there were many widows in Israel in Elijah's day, when heaven remained shut for three years and six months and a great famine raged throughout the land, but Elijah was not sent to any one of these, but only *to a widow at Zarephath, a town in Sidonia.* And there were many lepers in Israel in the prophet Elisha's time, but none of these was cured – only Naaman the Syrian.'

When they heard this everyone in the synagogue was enraged. They sprang to their feet and hustled him out of the town; and they took him up to the brow of the hill on which their town was built, intending to throw him off the cliff, but he passed through the midst of them and walked away.

Other readings: Jeremiah 1:4–5, 17–19 Psalm 70 (71)
1 Corinthians 12:31–13:13

THE STORY OF JESUS' visit to Nazareth, which we began reading last week, is placed by Luke at the very start of Jesus' ministry. The people are delighted by 'the words of grace' which he spoke. Quite suddenly, the atmosphere changes, and Jesus challenges the people's expectations. He knows that their approval is superficial. Prophets are generally rejected by their own.

Jesus illustrates this by referring to the two Old Testament prophets, Elijah and Elisha. Elijah encountered persecution in Israel and both prophets performed mighty works for those who were not Jews. Jesus stresses that the healing mercy of God is for all. The people of Nazareth react in annoyance, reject their own prophet and threaten physical violence.

Luke anticipates here the different reactions to the preaching of Jesus found in the rest of the gospel. Acceptance, rejection and violence will all be present.

What is my reaction to the preaching of Jesus?
Have I ever experienced being 'a prophet rejected by his own people'?
We ask that Jesus' words of grace will heal all bitterness and resentment.
We ask that we ourselves may be 'good news' to the stranger.

Fifth Sunday in Ordinary Time (Year C)

Luke 5:1–11

Now it happened that he was standing one day by the Lake of Gennesaret, with the crowd pressing round him listening to the word of God, when he caught sight of two boats at the water's edge. The fishermen had got out of them and were washing their nets. He got into one of the boats – it was Simon's – and asked him to put out a little from the shore. Then he sat down and taught the crowds from the boat.

When he had finished speaking he said to Simon, 'Put out into deep water and pay out your nets for a catch.' Simon replied, 'Master, we worked hard all night long and caught nothing, but if you say so, I will pay out the nets.' And when they had done this they netted such a huge number of fish that their nets began to tear, so they signalled to their companions in the other boat to come and help them; when these came, they filled both boats to sinking point.

When Simon Peter saw this he fell at the knees of Jesus saying, 'Leave me, Lord; I am a sinful man.' For he and all his companions were completely awestruck at the catch of fish they had made; so also were James and John, sons of Zebedee, who were Simon's partners. But Jesus said to Simon, 'Do not be afraid; from now on it is people you will be catching.' Then, bringing their boats back to land they left everything and followed him.

Other readings: Isaiah 6:1–8   Psalm 137 (138)   1 Corinthians 15:1–11

LUKE SOMETIMES PRESENTS THE gospel stories in a different order from Mark and Matthew. This is the case with this story of the call of the first disciples, which he places after the visits to Nazareth and Capernaum. The story is also fuller than the short accounts in Mark and Matthew. Jesus is preaching 'the word of God' when he gets into Simon's boat in order to teach the crowds from there. The miracle of the enormous catch of fish gives further background to the call of Simon Peter.

Luke makes clear that the disciples had already heard the preaching of Jesus and witnessed his miracles when they left everything to follow him. They respond 'at the Lord's word'. They 'hear the word and put it into practice'.

Simon Peter is deeply aware of his unworthiness, an echo of the call of the prophet Isaiah in the first reading. Jesus responds, 'Do not be afraid.' These words are heard repeatedly in the Scriptures when a person is called to take up a mission for God.

Does hearing the word of God make a difference in my life?
Am I able to trust the words of Christ 'Do not be afraid'?
Let us pray for the courage needed to respond to our vocation.
We ask for the wisdom, courage and love to be 'fishers of people'.

Sixth Sunday in Ordinary Time (Year C)

Luke 6:17, 20–26

He then came down with them and stopped at a piece of level ground where there was a large crowd of his disciples, with a great multitude of people from all parts of Judaea and Jerusalem and the coastal region of Tyre and Sidon who had come to hear him and to be cured of their diseases.

Then raising his eyes to his disciples he said:

'Blessed are you who are poor, for the kingdom of God is yours.

Blessed are you who are hungry now, for you shall be filled.

Blessed are you who are weeping now, for you shall laugh.

'Blessed are you when people hate you, drive you out,

abuse you, denounce your name as evil, on account of the Son of man. Rejoice when that day comes and leap for joy, see, your reward will be great in heaven. This was how their ancestors treated the prophets.

'But alas for you who are rich, for you are having your consolation now.

Alas for you who have plenty to eat now, for you shall go hungry.

Alas for you who are laughing now, for you shall mourn and weep.

Alas for you when everyone speaks well of you! For this was how their ancestors treated the false prophets.'

Other readings: Jeremiah 17:5–8   Psalm 1   1 Corinthians 15:12, 16–20

LUKE'S 'SERMON ON THE Plain' is much shorter than the more famous 'Sermon on the Mount' in Matthew's gospel. Both these collections of Jesus' teaching begin with beatitudes, introduced by 'blessed' or 'happy'. In Luke there are four, and they are followed by four 'woes', speeches which begin in our translation with 'alas'.

It is quite clear from the beatitudes that Jesus challenges the opinions of his own day, and indeed of ours. We encounter here the mystery which lies at the heart of the gospel and at the heart of life: that suffering and loss are an extraordinary channel of blessing. How difficult it is for Christians to fathom this truth! The loving self-sacrifice of Jesus on the cross is the best aid to reflecting on this mystery.

Jesus was sent to bring 'good news to the poor'. He will show repeatedly in Luke's gospel that lack of attachment to the good things of the world leaves a person free to discover the values of God. At the same time, to bring assistance to those in material poverty is a gospel imperative. When he speaks of the persecution of the prophets, and foresees the sufferings of Christians, Jesus points to his own fate.

In what sense is poverty a channel of blessing in my life?
How do I view the abuse people suffer for being Christian?
Let us pray for a profound detachment from material things.
Let us ask for courage and love in our dealings with those who deride us.

Seventh Sunday in Ordinary Time
(Year C)

Luke 6:27–38

Jesus said, 'But I say this to you who are listening: love your enemies, do good to those who hate you, bless those who curse you, pray for those who treat you badly. To anyone who slaps you on one cheek, present the other cheek as well; to anyone who takes your cloak from you, do not refuse your tunic. Give to everyone who asks you, and do not ask for your property back from someone who takes it. Treat others as you would like people to treat you. If you love those who love you, what credit is that to you? Even sinners love those who love them. And if you do good to those who do good to you, what credit is that to you? For even sinners do that much. And if you lend to those from whom you hope to receive, what credit is that to you? Even sinners lend to sinners to get back the same amount. Instead, love your enemies and do good to them, and lend without any hope of return. You will have a great reward, and you will be children of the Most High, for he himself is kind to the ungrateful and the wicked.

'Be compassionate just as your Father is compassionate. Do not judge, and you will not be judged; do not condemn, and you will not be condemned; forgive, and you will be forgiven. Give, and there will be gifts for you: a full measure, pressed down, shaken together, and overflowing, will be poured into your lap; because the standard you use will be the standard used for you.'

Other readings: 1 Samuel 26:2, 7–9, 12–13, 22–23   Psalm 102 (103)
1 Corinthians 15:45–49

WE CONTINUE READING FROM Luke's collection of the teaching of Jesus known as the 'Sermon on the Plain'. The essence of this reading is found in verses 27 and 28. There is a radical new teaching here given to all the disciples of Jesus, that we should love our enemies. This teaching is found in Matthew and Luke, in their respective collections of Jesus' teaching, and challenges the teaching of Jesus' contemporaries. This teaching is elaborated in the following verses, and repeated in verse 35. We are called to be like God, because we are children of God.

Throughout Luke's gospel Jesus reveals the compassion of God, and the call is for us to 'be compassionate as God is compassionate'. These are among the most difficult words of Jesus found anywhere in the four canonical gospels. The Christian is not called to 'do to others what you would want them to do to you', but, in a far more demanding manner, to 'do as God does'.

To what extent do I live the gospel command to 'love your enemies'?
Is compassion a major factor in my dealings with others?
Let us pray that we may truly imitate the love of Christ.
Let us pray for generosity of heart in all we do.

Eighth Sunday in Ordinary Time (Year C)

Luke 6:39–45

He also told them a parable, 'Can one blind person guide another? Surely both will fall into a pit? Disciple is not superior to teacher; but fully trained disciple will be like teacher. Why do you observe the splinter in another's eye and never notice the log in your own? How can you say to another, "My friend, let me take out that splinter in your eye," when you cannot see the log in your own? Hypocrite! Take the log out of your own eye first, and then you will see clearly to take out the splinter in another's eye.

'No good tree produces rotten fruit, nor again does a rotten tree produce good fruit, for every tree is known by its own fruit: people do not pick figs from thorns, nor gather grapes from a bramble. A good person brings out what is good from the store of goodness of the heart; an evil person draws out what is evil from the store of evil. For the mouth speaks from the overflow of the heart.'

Other readings: Ecclesiasticus 27:4–7 Psalm 91 (92) 1 Corinthians 15:54–58

WE CONTINUE READING FROM Luke's collection of the teaching of Jesus known as the 'Sermon on the Plain'. Jesus speaks first about the teacher and the disciple. If the teacher does not see clearly he will not be able to guide the disciple. And the disciple must respect his teacher, and be willing to learn.

We need clear sight for ourselves too. We tend to prefer correcting others to recognizing our own faults. We can be blind to so much in ourselves and still insist on correcting others. Once again, Jesus is stressing the need for the teacher to be a disciple first, to learn lessons, and then to give them.

The following verses speak of good and bad fruit. The teacher, and every faithful disciple, must produce good fruit. A good heart is necessary. This will be obvious when someone speaks, and, as the first reading from Ecclesiasticus maintains, conversation and speech are the 'test of men'.

Am I more willing to direct others than to learn for myself?
Do I fool myself with false judgements about myself?
Let us pray for honesty and humility, and a readiness to learn especially from the poor and the inadequate.
Let us seek always to speak with integrity.

Ninth Sunday in Ordinary Time (Year C)

Luke 7:1–10

When he had come to the end of all his sayings in the hearing of the people, he went into Capernaum. A centurion there had a servant, a favourite of his, who was sick and near death. Having heard about Jesus he sent some Jewish elders to him to ask him to come and heal his servant. When they came to Jesus they pleaded earnestly with him saying, 'He deserves this of you, because he loves our people, and he built us our synagogue himself.' So Jesus went with them, and was not far from the house when the centurion sent word by some friends to say to him, 'Lord, do not put yourself to any trouble because I am not worthy that you should come under my roof; and that is why I did not presume to come to you myself; but only speak a word and let my boy be cured. For I am under authority myself, and have soldiers under me; and I say to one man, "Go," and he goes; to another, "Come," and he comes; to my servant, "Do this," and he does it.' When Jesus heard these words he was astonished at him and, turning round, said to the crowd following him, 'I tell you, not even in Israel have I found faith as great as this.' And when the messengers got back to the house they found the servant in perfect health.

Other readings: 1 Kings 8:41–43   Psalm 116 (117)   Galatians 1:1–2, 6–10

THIS IS AN EXTRAORDINARY miracle story. Jesus meets neither the critically ill servant nor the centurion. It is a healing from a distance. In this healing, and in another such example of a healing from a distance, that of the daughter of the Canaanite woman recounted in Mark chapter 7, the beneficiaries are pagans. In both cases Jesus works a miracle for pagans but he observes Jewish custom and does not enter a Gentile house.

There are two sets of intermediaries who approach Jesus. The Jewish elders initially take the centurion's request to Jesus, and they are full of admiration for the pagan centurion. 'He loves our people,' they tell Jesus. He has generously funded the building of the synagogue. His goodness should be rewarded, they maintain.

The centurion changes his tactics half way through the story. As Jesus approaches the house, he sends 'friends' to tell Jesus that it will be quite enough to 'speak a word'. The centurion knows from experience that a command given out will be obeyed, and he considers that Jesus has similar power to command in his healing work. Furthermore, in sensitivity to Jewish custom regarding Gentiles, he expresses the conviction that Jesus does not need to enter his house.

The centurion's faith and his kindness are amply rewarded. The Gentile centurion becomes an example of faith, faith such as Jesus has not witnessed among the chosen people.

How supportive am I of the differing faith convictions of others?
How do I balance my fidelity to Christian faith with appreciation of the faith of others?

Let us pray for humility, and a readiness to listen to those of other
   cultural and religious traditions.
Let us recognise goodness wherever it is to be found.

Tenth Sunday in Ordinary Time (Year C)

Luke 7:11–17

It happened that soon afterwards he went to a town
called Nain, and disciples and a great number of people
accompanied him. Now when he was near the gate of the
town there was a dead man being carried out, the only son of
his mother, and she was a widow. And a considerable crowd
of the townspeople was with her. When the Lord saw her he
felt sorry for her and said to her, 'Don't cry.' Then he went up
and touched the bier and the bearers stood still, and he said,
'Young man, I tell you, get up.' And the dead man sat up and
began to talk, and Jesus *gave him to his mother*. Everyone was
filled with awe and glorified God saying, 'A great prophet has
been raised up among us; God has visited his people.' And
the word about him spread throughout Judaea and all over
the countryside.

Other readings: 1 Kings 17:17–24   Psalm 29 (30)   Galatians 1:11–19

THERE ARE ONLY A few accounts of the raising of the dead in the
four gospels. Matthew, Mark and Luke record the raising of the little
daughter of the synagogue official, Jairus. In John chapter 11 the
raising of Lazarus from the dead provokes growing antagonism to
Jesus as his death draws near. The raising of the son of the widow of
Nain in Luke's gospel has particular features. The evangelist stresses
the large number of people who witness this mighty deed and he
emphasises the compassion of Jesus. This woman is already a widow,
and now she has lost her only son, who presumably would have been
her only support.

The first words of Jesus are to the woman herself. He addresses her
with the simple command 'Do not cry.' In John chapter 20 the risen

Jesus says to Mary Magdalene 'Why are you weeping?' Tears shed at the loss of the beloved are wiped away by the joy of the resurrection. Jesus' words to the young man are brief and straightforward: 'Young man, I tell you to get up.' Literally, 'Young man, I tell you, be raised up.' When he raises the dead, Jesus points towards the resurrection.

Jesus' first concern continues to be for the mother: 'Jesus gave him to his mother.' He comes to confront sin and death, but also to heal the broken-hearted.

The reaction of the crowd is to proclaim Jesus a prophet. The raising of the young man by the prophet Elijah in the first Book of Kings is our first reading. In the verses following our gospel reading Luke records the question of the messengers sent by John the Baptist: 'Are you the one who is to come?' (7:20) Jesus replies: 'Go back and tell John what you have seen ... the dead are raised and the Good News is proclaimed to the poor.' (7:22)

Do I realise that the gospel is a message of life for all?
How might I reflect the compassion of Jesus in my life?
Pray for the bereaved, especially those who are without the support of family and friends.
Pray for those who care for the dying that they may do so with sensitivity and compassion.

Eleventh Sunday in Ordinary Time (Year C)

Luke 7:36–8:3

One of the Pharisees invited him to a meal. When he arrived at the Pharisee's house and took his place at table, suddenly a woman came in, who had a bad name in the town. She had heard he was dining in the Pharisee's house and had brought with her an alabaster jar of ointment. She waited behind him at his feet, weeping, and she began to bathe his feet with her tears, and she wiped them with her hair; then she covered his feet with kisses and anointed them with the ointment.

When the Pharisee who had invited him saw this, he said to himself, 'If this man were a prophet, he would know who this woman is and what sort of person it is who is touching him and what a bad name she has.' Then Jesus took him up and said, 'Simon, I have something to say to you.' He replied, 'Say on, teacher.' 'There was once a creditor who had two men in his debt; one owed him five hundred denarii, the other fifty. They were unable to pay, so he let them both off. Which of them will love him more?' Simon answered, 'The one who was let off more, I suppose.' Jesus said, 'You are right.'

Then he turned to the woman and said to Simon, 'You see this woman? I came into your house, and you poured no water over my feet, but she has bathed my feet with her tears and wiped them with her hair. You gave me no kiss, but she has been covering my feet with kisses ever since I came in. You did not anoint my head with oil, but she has anointed my feet with ointment. For this reason I tell you that her sins, many as they are, have been forgiven her, because she has shown such great love. One who is forgiven little, loves little.' Then he said to her, 'Your sins are forgiven.' Those who were with him at table began to say to themselves, 'Who is this man, that even forgives sins?' But he said to the woman, 'Your faith has saved you; go in peace.'

Now it happened that after this he made his way through towns and villages preaching and proclaiming the good news of the kingdom of God. With him went the Twelve, as well as certain women who had been cured of evil spirits and ailments: Mary surnamed the Magdalene, from whom seven demons had gone out, Joanna the wife of Herod's steward Chuza, Susanna, and many others who provided for them out of their own resources.

Other readings: 2 Samuel 12:7–10, 13 Psalm 31 (32) Galatians 2:16, 19–21

THIS READING IS CHARACTERISTIC of the Gospel of Luke, the gospel of the compassion of Christ. The focus of this story is on the woman's loving response to being forgiven. Awareness of God's forgiveness through the presence of Jesus leads her to demonstrate her love in an intimate way. The forgiveness of God in Christ cannot be earned by good works, but is freely given to those who are aware of their sin and seek it. Simon the Pharisee, despite his virtue, is less aware of his need for forgiveness, and consequently less loving. In Luke it is often the unlikely person who provides the most powerful example.

Luke also provides precious details about the women disciples of Jesus.

Am I aware of my need for forgiveness?
Do I realise that forgiveness can never be earned, but that it is freely given by God?
Pray for the gift of gratitude for God's patience and love.
Pray for those who see God as demanding and unforgiving.

Twelfth Sunday in Ordinary Time (Year C)

Luke 9:18–24

Now it happened that he was praying alone, and his disciples came to him and he put this question to them, 'Who do the crowds say I am?' And they answering said, 'Some say John the Baptist; others Elijah; others again that one of the ancient prophets has arisen.' He said to them, 'But you, who do you say I am?' In answer Peter said, 'The Messiah of God.' But he gave them strict orders and charged them not to say this to anyone, saying, 'The Son of man must suffer much, and be rejected by the elders and chief priests and scribes and be put to death, and on the third day be raised up.'

Then, speaking to all, he said, 'Anyone who wants to be a follower of mine, must renounce self and take up the cross every day and follow me. For whoever wants to save life will lose it; but whoever loses life for my sake, will save it.

Other readings: Zechariah 12:10–11; 13:1 Psalm 62 (63) Galatians 3:26–29

THIS READING WILL SOUND very familiar. The account of Peter's profession of faith is central to the three synoptic gospels, Matthew, Mark and Luke. Each evangelist presents this story in a way that fits in with his own way of narrating the gospel.

Luke reserves ten chapters of his gospel for the journey of Jesus from Galilee to Jerusalem. Later in chapter 9, from which today's gospel is taken, Jesus will set out on the road to Jerusalem, his journey to the cross and resurrection. Before this Jesus questions his disciples on their understanding of his mission, and gives his first warning to them that he is destined to suffer and die.

Peter's profession of faith in Jesus as the Messiah, the Christ, is told with great simplicity. As in the Gospel of Mark, Jesus' response is to command silence about his role. Jesus is unwilling to be drawn into popularity as the leader of a freedom movement. There is furthermore no commendation of Peter for his faith in Jesus, as appears when Matthew tells this story. Luke has other things to emphasise.

Jesus is called to give his life for others. This will be his path to new life. This path is to be followed not only by the disciples but by 'all'. For all of us the path to life will be marked by suffering, but Jesus has gone this way before us and he will bring us to the life of the resurrection. The scene is now set for Jesus to begin his journey to Jerusalem.

Who do you say Christ is?
Is it really possible to consider suffering as a gift?
Let us pray for those whose sufferings seem too hard to bear.
Let us pray for those who seek to alleviate the pain of others, whether physical or mental.

Thirteenth Sunday in Ordinary Time (Year C)

Luke 9:51–62

Now it happened that as the time drew near for him to be taken up, he resolutely turned his face towards Jerusalem and sent messengers ahead of him. These set out, and they went into a Samaritan village to make preparations for him, but the people would not receive him because he was making for Jerusalem. Seeing this, the disciples James and John said, 'Lord, do you want us to call down fire from heaven to burn them up?' But he turned and rebuked them, and they went on to another village.

As they were travelling along the road someone said to him, 'I will follow you wherever you go.' Jesus answered, 'Jackals have holes and the birds of the air have nests, but the Son of man has nowhere to lay his head.'

To another he said, 'Follow me.' But he replied, 'Let me first go and bury my father.' But he answered him, 'Leave the dead to bury their dead; but you go and proclaim the kingdom of God.'

Another said, 'I will follow you, Lord, but first let me go and say goodbye to my people at home.' Jesus said to him, 'No one who puts a hand to the plough and then looks back is fit for the kingdom of God.'

Other readings: 1 Kings 19:16, 19–21   Psalm 15 (16)   Galatians 5:1, 13–18

THIS GOSPEL READING MARKS a crucial point in the Gospel of Luke. It is the beginning of the journey of Jesus to Jerusalem, the place of his passion and death, and of his resurrection. The evangelist curiously speaks of the time for him to be 'taken up to heaven'. The journey is not simply the journey to death on the cross, but the journey to resurrection, which will culminate in the return of Jesus to the presence of the Father, from whom he came.

The rest of the gospel shows that the challenges faced by Jesus, the challenges of fidelity and hardship, will be faced by his disciples too. Unlike James and John, Jesus quietly accepts that the Samaritans, who no longer worshipped in Jerusalem, are unwilling to welcome him. Jesus warns the first man he meets of the privations of discipleship, that he has 'nowhere to lay his head'. His reply to the second man, that he should 'leave the dead to bury their dead', seems harsh. It is typical of the blunt language of the prophets, calculated to shake the listener out of complacency. Finally, Jesus challenges the third man's attachment to family ties. When all is considered, even these bonds of loyalty are secondary to the call of God. This final little scene echoes the conversation of the prophet Elijah with his disciple and successor Elisha in the first reading.

Am I prepared to make my journey to Jerusalem?
Is fidelity to the gospel the first priority in my life?
Pray for perseverance amid trials and hardships.
Pray for those who have no time for the good news.

Fourteenth Sunday in Ordinary Time (Year C)

Luke 10:1–12, 17–20

After this the Lord appointed seventy-two others and sent them out ahead of him in pairs, to all the towns and places where he intended to go. And he said to them, 'The harvest is rich but the labourers are few, so ask the Lord of the harvest to send out labourers to his harvest. Start off now, but look, I am sending you out like lambs among wolves. Take no purse with you, no bag, no sandals. Salute no one on the road. Whatever house you enter, let your first words be, "Peace to this house!" And if a person of peace lives there, your peace will rest on that person; if not, it will come back to you. Stay in the same house, taking what food and drink they have, for the labourer deserves to be paid; do not move from house to house. Whenever you go into a town where they make you welcome, eat what is put before you. Cure those in it who are sick, and say, "The kingdom of God has come near to you." But whenever you enter a town and they do not make you welcome, go out into its streets and say, "We wipe off the very dust of your town that clings to our feet, against you. Only be sure of this: the kingdom of God has come near to you." I tell you, on that day it will be more bearable for Sodom than for that town.'

The seventy-two came back rejoicing and saying, 'Lord, in your name even the demons submit to us.' He said to them, 'I watched Satan fall like lightning from heaven. Look, I have given you power to tread down serpents and scorpions and the whole strength of the enemy; nothing shall ever hurt you. Yet do not rejoice that spirits submit to you; rejoice instead that your names are written in heaven.'

Other readings: Isaiah 66:10–14   Psalm 65 (66)   Galatians 6:14–18

ONLY THE GOSPEL OF Luke gives this report of a sending out by Jesus of seventy-two (or seventy, in some manuscripts) disciples with the apparent task of preparing the way for his arrival. The number of disciples recalls Moses' appointment of elders to assist in his work reported in the book of Numbers (chapter 11). The logistics of the exercise are difficult to imagine, but the justification of it is clear. The harvest is rich, but the labourers are few. This has been a constant in the history of the Church, and is so in our day particularly due to the pressures of secularism and materialism which to many seem more attractive than labouring in the vineyard of Christ.

Jesus gives instructions as to how his disciples should behave. They are taught to provide little for themselves and to be single-minded. This seems to be the sense of the strange command to salute no one on the way. The salutation of 'peace' may be seen as encompassing the whole gospel message, which is to be imposed on no-one. They are told to remain in one house, avoiding any rivalry there might be among their hosts.

The announcement of 'peace', the peace of God, lies at the heart of the gospel, and is reflected in the words from Isaiah in the first reading 'Now towards her I send flowing peace, like a river.' These words are addressed to Jerusalem after the return of the people from exile in Babylon and they express the constant concern of the God who has not abandoned the people despite their sinfulness. The task of those called and sent by Jesus is precisely to bring the peace of God. They are to do this by proclaiming what Jesus proclaims, that the kingdom of God is near, and they are to confirm their message as Jesus did by acts of healing.

Am I single-minded in living the gospel?
How do I make the peace of the kingdom a reality for others?
Pray for an increase in labourers in the Lord's vineyard.
Thank God for the fidelity shown by so many in the work of the gospel.

Fifteenth Sunday in Ordinary Time (Year C)

Luke 10:25–37

And now a lawyer stood up and, to test him, asked, 'Teacher, what must I do to inherit eternal life?' He said to him, 'What is written in the Law? What is your reading of it?' He replied, '*You shall love the Lord your God with all your heart, with all your soul, with all your strength*, and with all your mind, *and your neighbour as yourself.*' Jesus said to him, 'You have answered right, do this and you shall live.'

But he was anxious to justify himself and said to Jesus, 'And who is my neighbour?' In answer Jesus said, 'A man was on his way down from Jerusalem to Jericho and fell into the hands of bandits; they stripped him, beat him and then made off, leaving him half dead. Now by chance a priest was travelling down the same road, but when he saw the man, he passed by on the other side. In the same way a Levite who came to the place saw him, and passed by on the other side. But a Samaritan traveller who came on him was moved with compassion when he saw him. He went up to him and bandaged his wounds, pouring oil and wine on them. He then lifted him onto his own mount and took him to an inn and looked after him. Next day, he took out two denarii and handed them to the innkeeper and said, "Look after him, and on my way back I will make good any extra expense." Which of these three, do you think, proved himself a neighbour to the man who fell into the bandits' hands?' He replied, 'The one who showed mercy towards him.' Jesus said to him, 'Go, and do the same yourself.'

**Other readings: Deuteronomy 30:10–14 Psalm 68 (69)
Colossians 1:15–20**

ONE OF THE EXTRAORDINARY features of the Gospel according to Luke is the presence of parables of Jesus only found in this gospel. The parable of the Good Samaritan is one of these. The parable is provoked by the question of the 'lawyer', an expert in the Jewish Law. The summary of the Law that he offers Jesus is the same as the reply

Jesus himself gives in other gospels. There is a profound agreement between Jesus and the experts on the Law.

To the lawyer's further question, 'And who is my neighbour?', Jesus replies not by entering into a dialogue about who and who is not a neighbour. For Jesus all people are to be treated as neighbours. Instead, Jesus tells a parable to illustrate how to behave as a neighbour to others. The painstaking compassion of the Samaritan for an unknown victim of violence in a hostile environment provides an example for all followers of Jesus.

In this story Jesus sets up as an example a Samaritan, one who belongs to a despised and hated race, considered heretical by the Jews, and contrasts him with two heartless religious professionals. The Samaritan, with his Christ-like behaviour, challenges every Christian.

Am I willing to learn from the example of those who are despised?
What do the words 'Go and do the same yourself' ask of me today?
Pray for those involved in bringing assistance to the victims of violence,
    terrorism and war.
Pray for harmony among people of different religious beliefs.

Sixteenth Sunday in Ordinary Time (Year C)

Luke 10:38-42

In the course of their journey he came to a village, and a woman named Martha welcomed him into her house. She had a sister called Mary, who sat down at the Lord's feet and listened to him speaking. Now Martha, who was distracted with all the serving, came to him and said, 'Lord, do you not care that my sister is leaving me to do the serving all by myself? Then tell her to help me.' But the Lord answered, 'Martha, Martha,' he said, 'you worry and fret about so many things, and yet few are needed, indeed only one. It is Mary who has chosen the better part, and it is not to be taken from her.'

Other readings: Genesis 18:1-10   Psalm 14 (15)   Colossians 1:24-28

ONCE MORE IN THIS Sunday's gospel we have material only found in the Gospel according to Luke. Jesus began his journey to Jerusalem to face his death in the previous chapter. He now reaches a village where he will receive generous hospitality. Luke has placed this story at an early stage of the journey. This raises a question for we know from the Gospel of John that Martha and Mary lived in the village of Bethany quite close to Jerusalem. This does not of course undermine the accuracy and the validity of the story itself.

Luke underlines the presence of women in the ministry of Jesus. In chapter 8 he listed some of the women disciples who accompanied Jesus together with the Twelve. In chapter 7 Jesus was the recipient of the tender attention of the woman who had been a sinner. In our passage Jesus comes to the house of two women.

The heart of the story lies in the contrast between the attitudes and actions of Mary and Martha. Mary somehow understands how precious the words of Jesus are. Everything else is of little importance. She has fathomed one of the most important teachings of this gospel, the need to hear the word of the Lord. They are blessed who hear the word of God and practise it (11:28).

Martha on the other hand is intent on the practical concerns of providing hospitality for her guest. In the very first verse the evangelist tells us that it is Martha who welcomes Jesus into the house. Martha takes charge, but she prefers action to quiet listening. Jesus is a guest to be served, rather than a teacher whose every word is to be learned and treasured.

The mild rebuke of Jesus is for those who do not make the time for what is of the utmost importance, listening to his words. From the very start of his gospel, with the Annunciation to Mary, Luke has stressed that our primary concern should be to hear the words of the Lord.

Do I treasure the word of God and take steps to hear and practise it?
Do I have the priorities of a genuine disciple of Jesus?
We pray for those whose vocation is to listen.
We pray that our service may always be inspired by love.

Seventeenth Sunday in Ordinary Time (Year C)

Luke 11:1–13

Now it happened that he was in a certain place praying, and when he had finished, one of his disciples said, 'Lord, teach us to pray, as John taught his disciples.' He said to them, 'When you pray, this is what to say:

'Father, may your name be held holy,
your kingdom come;
give us each day our daily bread,
and forgive us our sins,
for we ourselves forgive everyone who is in debt to us.
And do not put us to the test.'

He also said to them, 'Suppose one of you has a friend and goes to him in the middle of the night to say, "My friend, lend me three loaves, because a friend of mine on his travels has just arrived at my house and I have nothing to put before him;" and the man answers from inside the house, "Do not bother me. The door is bolted now, and my children are with me in bed; I cannot get up to give it to you." I tell you, if the man does not get up and give it to him for friendship's sake, persistence will make him get up and give his friend all he needs.

'So I say to you: ask, and it will be given to you; search, and you will find; knock, and the door will be opened to you. For everyone who asks receives; everyone who searches finds; everyone who knocks will have the door opened. What father among you, if his son asked for a fish, would hand him a snake? Or if he asked for an egg, hand him a scorpion? If you then, evil as you are, know how to give your children what is good, how much more will the heavenly Father give the Holy Spirit to those who ask him!'

Other readings: Genesis 18:20–32 Psalm 137 (138) Colossians 2:12–14

THE OVERRIDING THEME OF this passage is the compassion and loving-kindness of the Father. Much of the material in this rather long gospel reading is found also in the Gospel of Matthew, as part of the Sermon on the Mount. The compassion of God is a major theme of the preaching of Jesus.

The first section is the shorter form of the Lord's Prayer. Prayer for the coming of the Kingdom and for all we need to journey towards it are the essential elements. The parable of the friend who comes by night follows. It teaches perseverance in prayer. In the final section we are taught to put that teaching into practice. The fatherly love of God surpasses all human fatherhood. If human beings, prone to sin as they are, know how to care for their children, how much more can we expect from the God who is holy and who bestows the Holy Spirit on receptive souls!

Do I trust in the fatherly love of God, or does failed human love cloud my vision?
In what sense do those who ask always receive?
We pray for those who struggle to believe in the goodness of God.
We pray for those who promote false images of God.

Eighteenth Sunday in Ordinary Time (Year C)

Luke 12:13–21

A man in the crowd said to him, 'Teacher, tell my brother to give me a share of our inheritance.' He said to him, 'My friend, who appointed me judge or arbitrator over you?' Then he said to them, 'Watch, and be on your guard against avarice of any kind, for life does not consist in abundance of possessions.'

Then he told them a parable, 'There was once a rich man who, having had a good harvest from his land, thought to himself, "What am I to do? I have not enough room to store my crops." Then he said, "This is what I will do: I will pull down my barns and build bigger ones, and store all my grain and my goods in them. And I will say to my soul: my soul, you have plenty of good things laid by for many years to come; take things easy, eat, drink, have a good time." But God said to him, "Fool! This very night the demand will be made for your soul; and this hoard of yours, whose will it be then?" So it is when someone stores up treasure for himself instead of becoming rich with regard to God.'

**Other readings: Ecclesiastes 1:2; 2:21–23   Psalm 89 (90)
Colossians 3:1–5, 9–11**

ONE OF THIS EVANGELIST'S major interests is the teaching of Jesus about riches and poverty. The parable of the rich fool, which illustrates the corrupting influence and foolishness of wealth, is found only in the Gospel of Luke. It is provoked by the question of a man who is anxious to get his hands on his inheritance.

The warning of Jesus is against 'avarice'. The Greek word *pleonexia* means literally the craving for more. Possessions do not guarantee life. In the parable the rich man has no consideration for the needs of others, despite the fact that he has more than he could ever need. This parable recalls Jesus' words earlier in the gospel, when he declared the poor blessed, and the rich cursed (Luke 6).

God calls the rich man 'Fool!' reminding us that the gospel is the ultimate answer to the human search for wisdom. Rejection of it is rejection of the true path to God and to life. Fulness of life comes not from possessions, which are, in the words of Ecclesiastes, 'vanity of vanities', but from the discovery of the trustworthy God of the poor.

The lesson in each of today's Scripture readings is of enormous relevance to the world of today, both developed and developing, in which desperate poverty is so often found alongside extraordinary wastefulness and extravagance. In the reading from the Letter to the Colossians St Paul describes greed as 'worshipping a false god'.

Do I allow the craving for more to control my life or my decisions?
In what sense do those who ask always receive?
We pray for those who are trapped by their own addictions and desires.
We pray for the gift of true freedom.

Nineteenth Sunday in Ordinary Time (Year C)

Luke 12:32–48

Jesus said, 'There is no need to be afraid, little flock, for it has pleased your Father to give you the kingdom. Sell your possessions and give alms. Get yourselves purses that do not wear out, an unfailing treasure in heaven, where no thief comes near and no moth destroys. For where your treasure is, that is where your heart will be too.

'See that you have your belts done up and your lamps lit. Be like people waiting for their master to return from the wedding feast, ready to open the door as soon as he comes and knocks. Blessed are those servants whom the master finds awake when he comes. Amen I say to you, he will do up his belt, sit them down at table and wait on them. He may come in the middle of the night or when it is nearly dawn, but blessed are those servants if he finds them ready.

'You may be sure of this, that if the householder had known at what time the burglar would come, he would not have let anyone break through the wall of his house. You too must stand ready, because the Son of man is coming at an hour you do not expect.'

Peter said, 'Lord, do you mean this parable for us, or for everyone?' The Lord replied, 'Who, then, is the wise and trustworthy steward whom the master will place over his household to give them at the proper time their allowance of food? Blessed is that servant if his master's arrival finds him doing exactly that. I tell you truly, he will put him in charge of everything that he owns. But if the servant says to himself, "My master is taking his time coming," and sets about beating the menservants and the servant-girls, and eating and drinking and getting drunk, his master will come on a day he does not expect and at an hour he does not know. The master will cut him off and send him to the same fate as unbelievers.

'The servant who knows what the master wants, but has got nothing ready and done nothing in accord with those wishes, will be given a great many strokes of the lash. The one who did not know, but has acted in a way to deserve a beating, will be given fewer strokes. When someone is given a great deal, a great deal will be demanded of that person; when someone is entrusted with a great deal, of that person even more will be expected.

Other readings: Wisdom 18:6–9 Psalm 32 (33) Hebrews 11:1–2, 8–19

THE THEME OF READINESS for the coming of the Lord is generally to be found towards the end of the gospel story. This is clearly so in the gospels of Mark (chapter 13) and Matthew (chapters 24 and 25). In Matthew's gospel the parable of the wise and foolish virgins describes the readiness of the wise virgins, who have brought oil with their lamps, to welcome the bridegroom. Here in Luke Jesus is still journeying to Jerusalem when he encourages all disciples to be ready with their lamps lit to welcome the return of the master from the wedding feast.

The disciple-servant must be ready for the return of the master, who will come and knock at the door. Such servants are declared blessed, but, in a surprising reversal, it is the master who waits on the servants. This recalls the story of the washing of the feet of the disciples by Jesus in John's gospel (chapter 13).

Jesus is described as the servant throughout the gospels. In Luke's gospel he says to the disciples at the Last Supper: 'Yet here am I among you as one who serves!' (Luke 22:27).

The theme of constant readiness is developed by reference to the times of the night. The lateness of the hour underlines the sacrifice required of the servant in staying alert to welcome the master. A further short parable follows: the idea of a house being plundered once again encourages watchfulness.

The reading from the Book of Wisdom describes how the Israelites waited for deliverance on the night of the Passover. Christians have already experienced the saving death and resurrection of the Lord. Now we await his return.

Would it be accurate to say that I have my lamp lit to go out and meet the Lord?
Am I prepared to persevere in the life of faith with joy and hope?
We pray for courage for Christians who struggle with their faith.
We pray for the coming of the Lord.

Twentieth Sunday in Ordinary Time (Year C)

Luke 12:49–53

Jesus said, 'I have come to bring fire to the earth, and how I wish it were already lit! There is a baptism I must still receive, and what constraint I am under until it is completed! Do you suppose that I am here to bring peace on earth? No, I tell you, but rather division. For from now on, a household of five will be divided: three against two and two against three; *father opposed to son*, son to father, mother to daughter, *daughter to mother*, mother-in-law to daughter-in-law, *daughter-in-law to mother-in-law*.'

Other readings: Jeremiah 38:4–6, 8–10   Psalm 39 (40)   Hebrews 12:1–4

THE WORDS OF JESUS in the gospel can sometimes be quite shocking. How is it possible to believe that Jesus has come to bring not peace, but conflict? The prophet Jesus uses blunt and challenging language. His words convey a profound truth, for the consequence of his preaching will be division, even within families. His uncompromising preaching about God and human life produces opposition and division, which both Jesus and his followers have to face.

Fire is nevertheless a disturbing image. It is used in the Jewish Scriptures to symbolise punishment and destruction. Jesus is using the strong language common among his contemporaries to speak of the judgement of God in stark terms. He speaks also of his coming baptism. In Christian baptism we undergo a kind of dying in order to reach new life. Baptism for Jesus is the baptism of the cross, his death leading to resurrection. Jesus is anxious to continue his journey to Jerusalem and to complete his mission.

Jesus explicitly says he has not come to bring peace. These words speak of the inevitable consequence of his message. Divisions are foreseen, and divisions and conflicts have been a constant reality because the Christian gospel makes great demands. The challenge is to continue to speak the truth with love in spite of opposition.

The reading about the prophet Jeremiah which accompanies this gospel illustrates the persecution often faced by the prophets. Jeremiah's intentions are misrepresented: he 'does not have the welfare of this people at heart'. He is thrown into a well and sinks into the mud. He is eventually rescued by someone who is willing to stand with him and risk persecution himself. As the Letter to the Hebrews says, we are supported by 'a great cloud of witnesses' as we continue the race of faith which we have begun.

Am I willing to speak the truth even when it might cause
  unpleasantness?
Am I prepared to suffer for my faith?
We pray for those who preach the good news despite opposition and
  persecution.
We pray for peace in the Church and in the world.

Twenty-first Sunday in Ordinary Time (Year C)

Luke 13:22–30

Through towns and villages he went teaching, making his way to Jerusalem. Someone said to him, 'Sir, will there be only a few saved?' He said to them, 'Strive to enter by the narrow door, because, I tell you, many will try to enter and will not succeed.

'Once the master of the house has got up and locked the door, you may find yourself standing outside knocking on the door, saying, "Lord, open to us," but he will answer, "I do not know where you come from." Then you will start saying, "We once ate and drank in your company; you taught in our streets," but he will reply, "I do not know where you come from; *away from me, all evil doers!*" Then there will be weeping and gnashing of teeth, when you see Abraham and Isaac and Jacob and all the prophets in the kingdom of God, and yourselves thrown out. And people from east and west, from north and south, will come and sit down at the feast in the kingdom of God.

'Look, there are those now last who will be first, and those now first who will be last.'

Other readings: Isaiah 66:18–21   Psalm 116 (117)   Hebrews 12:5–7, 11–13

THIS GOSPEL READING COMBINES two themes: the difficulty of entering the kingdom of God, and the arrival of people from every corner of the earth. Will it be easy to enter the kingdom? No! Can we determine beforehand who will enter the kingdom? No!

The gospel begins with a tricky theological question posed to Jesus. Will there be only a few saved? Jesus does not give a direct answer. It is not for us to know such things. It is for each one to strive for the kingdom, realising that there is nothing of greater importance.

Jesus then speaks of the danger of presuming to be saved. Those who do so may find themselves barred from the kingdom. There is a clear implication here that simply to have heard and known about Jesus is not enough. The patriarchs and prophets of God's faithful people will be admitted, together with all those people from north, south, east and west who have responded to the call of God. The call does not guarantee salvation. Whether we are Jew or Gentile, it is our response that matters.

Do I presume that the way to the kingdom of God will be easy?
Do I have fixed ideas about who will enter the kingdom of God?
Let us pray for those who have lost all desire to find God in their lives.
Let us pray for a deeper sense of belonging to the Church throughout the world.

Twenty-second Sunday in Ordinary Time (Year C)

Luke 14:1, 7–14

Now it happened that on a Sabbath he had gone to share a meal in the house of one of the leading Pharisees; and they watched him closely.

He then told the guests a parable, because he had noticed how they picked the places of honour. He said this, 'When someone invites you to a wedding feast, do not take your seat in the place of honour, in case a more distinguished person than you has been invited, and the person who invited you both may come and say, "Give up your place to this person." And then, to your embarrassment, you will have to go and take the lowest place. No; when you are invited, make your way to the lowest place and sit there, so that, when your host comes, he may say, "My friend, move up higher." Then, everyone with you at the table will see you honoured. For everyone who raises himself up will be humbled, and the one who humbles himself will be raised up.'

Then he said to his host, 'When you give a lunch or a dinner, do not invite your friends or your brothers or sisters or your relations or rich neighbours, in case they invite you back and so repay you. No; when you have a party, invite the poor, the crippled, the lame, the blind; then you will be blessed, for they have no means to repay you, and so you will be repaid at the resurrection of the righteous.'

Other readings: Ecclesiasticus 3:17-20, 28-29   Psalm 67 (68)
Hebrews 12:18-19, 22-24

THIS GOSPEL ILLUSTRATES HOW Jesus, as an astute teacher, used the situations in which he found himself to challenge people. In this case his teaching is about the right attitude to have as a guest, and as a host. It is not surprising that the Old Testament reading chosen to reflect the gospel is from the Book of Ecclesiasticus, one of the so-called Wisdom books. These books do not hesitate to give direct advice about the way to behave properly. The reading from Ecclesiasticus today is about humility.

Jesus takes up the traditions of the Jewish teachers of wisdom. So what is new about his teaching here? He brings with him the traditional teaching and confirms it, but he also lives it, not simply by his own everyday behaviour, but by going to the lowest place in accepting his martyrdom on the cross. These apparently mundane teachings, which are set during his journey to Jerusalem to face death, remind us of his willingness to be the servant of all and to give up his life. As he makes his way to Jerusalem the servant Jesus teaches us how to be truly servants, and the humble

Jesus teaches us how to be truly humble. For the Christian there is nothing too mundane, no activity which cannot benefit from the light of faith. For the Christian there is no person who does not deserve the gift of our hospitality, the gift of our love.

Do I endeavour to shed the light of faith on all my actions and decisions?

Do I strive for true humility in my attitudes and behaviour?

Let us pray for a heart that is welcoming towards those who are rejected and ill-treated.

Let us pray that despite our weakness we may one day take our place at the wedding feast of God.

Twenty-third Sunday in Ordinary Time (Year C)

Luke 14:25–33

Great crowds accompanied him on his way and he turned and spoke to them. 'Anyone who comes to me without hating father, mother, wife, children, brothers, sisters, yes and even life itself, cannot be my disciple. No one who fails to carry the cross and come after me can be my disciple. And indeed, which of you here, intending to build a tower, would not first sit down and work out the cost to see if you had enough to complete it? Otherwise, if you laid the foundation and then found yourself unable to finish the work, anyone who saw it would start making fun of you and saying, "Here is someone who started to build and was unable to finish." Or again, what king marching to war against another king would not first sit down and consider whether with ten thousand men he could stand up to the other who was advancing against him with twenty thousand? If not, then while the other king was still a long way off, he would send envoys to negotiate peace. So in the same way, none of you can be my disciple without giving up all that you own.'

Other readings: Wisdom 9:13–18 Psalm 89 (90) Philemon 9–10, 12–17

THE START OF THIS GOSPEL reading should remind us that Jesus is on his way to Jerusalem. Luke tells us that many people were willing to follow him. His journey from Galilee to Jerusalem began in chapter 9. It is a journey to face the cross and is filled with teaching for those who are willing to take up their crosses as disciples of Jesus.

Once again Jesus uses the stark language of the prophets. To hate one's closest relatives should not be interpreted literally, but in the sense of preferring nothing and nobody to following Jesus.

The second section of the gospel concerns prudence. Jesus tells two short parables, about the man building the tower, and another about a king going to war. Discipleship involves both the heart and the mind. We need to count the cost of discipleship. There is an apparent contradiction here for the passage ends with another radical statement of Jesus: 'None of you can be my disciple unless he gives up all his possessions.' Each person must calculate the cost and give what God inspires through heart and mind. God does not demand what is impossible for a person to give. Detachment is the key.

The first reading praises the gift of Wisdom, which comes from God. Jesus is this true Wisdom, who guides, inspires and challenges us on the road to the fulness of life.

Do I manage to put God above all else in my life?
Do I use my intelligence to make decisions about discipleship?
Let us pray for the gift of the Holy Spirit to guide our
detachment to generosity.
Let us pray for courage in following Jesus to Jerusalem, to the
cross and to new life.

Twenty-fourth Sunday in Ordinary Time (Year C)

Luke 15:1–32

The tax collectors and sinners, however, were all crowding round to listen to him, and the Pharisees and scribes complained saying, 'This man welcomes sinners and eats with them.' So he told them this parable.

'Which one of you with a hundred sheep, if he loses one, does not leave the ninety-nine in the desert and go after the missing one till he finds it? And when he has found it, he puts it on his shoulders rejoicing, and when he gets home, calls together his friends and neighbours, saying to them, "Rejoice with me, I have found my sheep that was lost." In the same way, I tell you, there will be more rejoicing in heaven over one sinner repenting than over ninety-nine righteous people who have no need of repentance.

'Or again, what woman with ten silver coins would not, if she lost one, light a lamp and sweep out the house and search thoroughly till she found it? And then, when she had found it, call together her friends and neighbours, saying to them, "Rejoice with me, I have found the silver coin I lost." In the same way, I tell you, there is rejoicing in the presence of the angels of God over one repentant sinner.'

Then he said, 'There was a man who had two sons. The younger one said to his father, "Father, let me have the share of the estate that will come to me." So the father divided the property between them. A few days later, the younger son got together everything he had and left for a distant country where he squandered his money in loose living.

'When he had spent it all, that country experienced a severe famine, and now he began to be in need; so he hired himself out to one of the local inhabitants who sent him into the fields to feed the pigs. And he would willingly have filled himself with the pods which the pigs were eating, but no one would let him have them. Then he came to his senses and said, "How many of my father's hired men have all the food they want and more, and here am I dying of hunger! I will get up and go to my father and say: Father, I have sinned against heaven and against you; I no longer deserve to be called your son; treat me as one of your hired men." So he got up and went back to his father.

'While he was still a long way off, his father saw him and was moved with pity. He ran to the boy, clasped him in his arms and kissed him. Then his son said, "Father, I have sinned against heaven and against you. I no longer deserve to be called your son." But the father said to his servants, "Quick! Bring out the best robe and put it on him; put a ring on his finger and sandals on his feet. Bring the fattened calf, and kill it; we will celebrate by having a feast, because this son of mine was dead and has come back to life; he was lost and is found." And they began to celebrate.

'Now the elder son was out in the fields, and on his way back, as he drew near the house, he heard music and dancing. Calling one of the servants he asked what it was all about. The servant told him, "Your brother has come, and your father has killed the fattened calf because he has got him back safe and sound." He was angry then and refused to go in, and his father came out and began to plead with him; but he retorted to his father, "Look! All these years I have slaved for you and never disobeyed your orders, yet you never gave me so much as a young goat for me to celebrate with my friends. But, for this son of yours, when he comes back after swallowing up your property with prostitutes you kill the fattened calf." Then the father said, "My son, you are with me always and all I have is yours. But it was only right we should celebrate and rejoice, because your brother here was dead and has come to life; he was lost and is found."'

Other readings: Exodus 32:7-11, 13-14 Psalm 50 (51) 1 Timothy 1:12-17

CHAPTER 15 OF THE Gospel of Luke contains three parables: the parables of the lost sheep, the lost coin and the prodigal son. The parable of the prodigal son was read this year on the Fourth Sunday of Lent.

The evangelist gathers these three parables together because they all teach us about the joy of God at the repentance of the sinner. The opening verses tell us about those among Jesus' hearers who were severely critical of his welcome to sinners. They 'complained'. The Greek word in the original text of the gospel also means 'grumble'. Those who complain here are like the elder brother in the parable of the prodigal son who refuses to join the celebration of his younger brother's return.

The first two parables are rather startling. Would a shepherd really leave the care of ninety-nine sheep to search for one? Would a woman who found a lost coin really put on a feast to celebrate? The lack of realism in these parables teaches us that God's behaviour goes far beyond human normality. God forgives in an outstanding way. In giving us a Saviour God shows a love far beyond any human love. The scribes and Pharisees found the forgiving love of God hard to accept. But what about us?

Do I rejoice at the return of the sinner or consider God to be soft?
Do I try to stretch my heart and mind to grasp the extraordinary ways
*   of God?*
Let us pray for those who grumble at the forbearance of God.
Let us pray for those trying to find forgiveness.

Twenty-fifth Sunday in Ordinary Time (Year C)

Luke 16:1–13

He also said to his disciples, 'There was a rich man and he had a manager who was denounced to him for squandering his property. He called for the man and said, "What is this I hear about you? Draw me up an account of your management because you are not to be my manager any longer." Then the manager said to himself, "Now that my master is taking my position away from me, what am I to do? I am not strong enough to dig. I would be ashamed to go begging. I know what I will do to make sure that when I am dismissed from office people will welcome me into their homes."

'Then he called his master's debtors one by one. To the first he said, "How much do you owe my master?" "One hundred jars of oil," he said. The manager said, "Take your bond; sit down and quickly write fifty." To another he said, "And you, sir, how much do you owe?" "One hundred sacks of wheat," he said. The manager said, "Take your bond and write eighty." The master praised the dishonest manager for his astuteness. For the children of this world are more astute in dealing with their own kind than are the children of light.

'And so I tell you this: use money, tainted as it is, to win you friends, and thus make sure that when it fails you, they will welcome you into eternal dwellings. Anyone who is trustworthy in the smallest matters is trustworthy in great; anyone who is dishonest in the smallest matters is dishonest in great. If then you have not been trustworthy with money, that tainted thing, who will trust you with genuine riches? And if you are not trustworthy with what is not yours, who will give you what is your very own?

'No servant can serve two masters: a servant will either hate the first and love the second, or be attached to the first and despise the second. You cannot serve both God and money.'

Other readings: Amos 8:4–7 Psalm 112 (113) 1 Timothy 2:1–8

THE PARABLE OF THE dishonest manager, with which the reading begins, is perhaps the most difficult of all the parables of Jesus. How could Jesus suggest to us as an example a man who is clearly dishonest? The answer to this question comes in verse 8, at the conclusion of the parable, when the manager's master praises him 'for his astuteness'. We are not called to imitate the man's dishonesty, demonstrated both before and after his dismissal, but his shrewdness. The manager quickly grasps how desperate his situation is and immediately seeks a solution. Jesus challenges us to do the same.

The final verses concern the proper use of money. They urge us to be trustworthy 'in the smallest matters' as well as great. We are challenged to be slaves of God, not of material things. Luke places these verses here to ensure we do not misunderstand the parable of the dishonest manager.

Do I really understand the urgency of the call of Jesus?
Am I willing to learn from 'the children of this world'?
Let us pray that we may shake off our lethargy and behave as 'children of the light'.
Let us resolve to be honest in little things as well as great.

Twenty-sixth Sunday in Ordinary Time (Year C)

Luke 16:19–31

Jesus said, 'There was a rich man who used to dress in purple and fine linen and feast magnificently every day. And at his gate there used to lie a poor man called Lazarus, covered with sores, who longed to fill himself with what fell from the rich man's table. Even dogs came and licked his sores. Now it happened that the poor man died and was carried away by the angels into Abraham's embrace. The rich man also died and was buried. In his torment in Hades he looked up and saw Abraham a long way off with Lazarus in his embrace. So he cried out, "Father Abraham, have mercy on me and send Lazarus to dip the tip of his finger in water and cool my tongue, for I am in agony in these flames." Abraham said, "My son, remember that during your life you had your fill of good things, just as Lazarus his fill of bad. Now he is being comforted here while you are in agony. But that is not all: between us and you a great gulf has been fixed, to block those who want to cross from our side to yours or from your side to ours." So he said, "Father, I beg you then to send Lazarus to my father's house, since I have five brothers, to give them warning so that they do not come to this place of torment too." Abraham said, "They have Moses and the prophets, let them listen to them." The rich man replied, "Ah no, father Abraham, but if someone comes to them from the dead, they will repent." Then Abraham said to him, "If they will not listen either to Moses or to the prophets, they will not be convinced even if someone should rise from the dead." '

Other readings: Amos 6:1, 4–7   Psalm 145 (146)   1 Timothy 6:11–16

ONCE AGAIN WE HEAR a parable which is only recorded by the evangelist Luke. It is a high point of the social teaching of Jesus. He points to the desperate injustice of one man's treatment of another, a theme which is as relevant today as it was then.

The profound disregard which the rich man shows to

the poor man at his very gate should give us all a jolt. Is it possible we too perpetrate such injustice? The parable makes very clear that the time for action is now. The day will come when the 'great gulf' will be fixed and we will no longer be able to assist our fellow human beings in their need.

The rich man from Hades continues to look on Lazarus as his inferior. He asks Abraham to send Lazarus to warn his brothers to repent. But the warning is already to be found in the words of the Scriptures, in the Law and in prophets such as Amos.

Does the parable have anything to say to me here and now?
Am I sufficiently committed to working for a better world?
Let us pray for the eyes to see the needs of others and the heart
*   to respond.*
Let us pray for justice and solidarity in human affairs.

Twenty-seventh Sunday in Ordinary Time (Year C)

Luke 17:5-10

The apostles said to the Lord, 'Increase our faith.' The Lord replied, 'If you had faith the size of a mustard seed you could say to this mulberry tree, "Be uprooted and planted in the sea," and it would obey you.

'Which of you, who had a servant ploughing or minding sheep, would say to him when he returned from the fields, "Come and have your meal at once"? Would he not be more likely to say, "Get my supper ready; fasten your belt and wait on me while I eat and drink. You yourself can eat and drink afterwards"? Must he be grateful to the servant for obeying orders? So with you: when you have done all you have been told to do, say, "We are useless servants: we have done no more than our duty." '

Other readings: Habakkuk 1:2-3, 2:2-4 Psalm 94 (95)
2 Timothy 1:6-8, 13-14

WE CONTINUE READING TEACHINGS of Jesus as he makes his way to Jerusalem. There are two themes in these verses: faith and service. In both cases Jesus seems to be giving a warning about great expectations in the life of discipleship. We are not called upon to be high achievers in the life of faith and love.

We are not told why the apostles suddenly ask Jesus to help their lack of faith. Jesus' reply is striking and hardly encouraging. The mustard seed, as Jesus teaches elsewhere, is the smallest of the seeds. Astonishingly, Jesus implies that the apostles do not have faith even that small. If they did, then they could do extraordinary wonders. Perhaps what Jesus is teaching is that faith is part of a completely different order, in which different rules apply. The desire for faith, the sense that one's faith needs to increase, is already something precious. The presence of God in a person's life is more important than striving for a deeper faith.

A short parable follows. The true disciple is to look upon himself as a 'useless servant'. This would surely have sounded strange to many of the disciples of Jesus. Once again the words of Jesus are challenging. Is it right that we should consider whatever we do simply as a duty? The point here is to realise that God does not demand huge achievements from us. To seek to serve is all that is necessary, for Jesus himself came to serve and not to be served. The love of God in a person's life is far more important than striving for great achievements even in the service of God.

Does faith in God lie at the very heart of my life?
Am I content to be a 'useless servant'?
Let us pray for openness to the words of Jesus, especially when they
    challenge us and perplex us.
Let us pray for the gifts of true faith and true love.

Twenty-eighth Sunday in Ordinary Time (Year C)

Luke 17:11–19

Now it happened that on the way to Jerusalem he was travelling in the borderlands of Samaria and Galilee. As he entered one of the villages, ten men suffering from leprosy came to meet him. They stood some way off and called to him, 'Jesus! Master! Have mercy on us.' When he saw them he said, 'Go and show yourselves to the priests.' Now as they were going away they were cleansed. Finding himself cured, one of them turned back praising God at the top of his voice and threw himself prostrate at the feet of Jesus and thanked him. The man was a Samaritan. This led Jesus to say, 'Were not ten made clean? The other nine, where are they? Was none of them found to come back to give praise to God, except this foreigner?' And he said to the man, 'Stand up and go on your way. Your faith has saved you.'

Other readings: 2 Kings 5:14–17   Psalm 97 (98)   2 Timothy 2:8–13

THIS STORY OF THE healing of the ten lepers is unique to the Gospel of Luke. It takes place as Jesus continues his journey to Jerusalem. The ten lepers, people with a virulent skin disease who due to its contagious nature were not allowed to live in the village, had obviously heard of the powerful healings of Jesus. They 'stood some way off' and called out.

In Luke chapter 5 Jesus had touched and healed a leper. In this case he does not heal the lepers straightaway but rather sends them off to report their state of 'uncleanness' to the priests. Jesus is respecting the religious rules of Judaism, but the lepers never reach the priests since 'as they were going away they were cleansed'.

The second part of the story concerns gratitude for God's healing. Only the Samaritan shows gratitude for his healing. In the parable of the Good Samaritan Jesus had set a Samaritan before us as an example of love of neighbour. The Samaritans were despised by the Jews due to religious differences, and yet it is the Samaritan who is the only one of the ten to show gratitude and praise God for his healing. Jesus asks: 'The other nine, where are they?'

The man who was doubly an outcast, due to his sickness and due to his race, hears the words of salvation: 'your faith has saved you'. Is the evangelist implying that the fulness of salvation was not given to the other nine? They received an extraordinary gift from Jesus, healing of the body which was a sign of the coming Kingdom of God, but they did not understand the sign and showed no gratitude for it. They received God's gifts without acknowledging the giver. Is gratitude then essential for salvation?

Am I truly grateful for the gifts of God?
Am I willing to see the goodness of God in those who are despised?
Let us pray for courage in the face of illness and disease.
Let us pray for those who care for the sick, and those who offer healing.

Twenty-ninth Sunday in Ordinary Time (Year C)

Luke 18:1–8

Then he told them a parable about the need to pray continually and never lose heart. He said, 'There was a judge in a certain town, who had neither fear of God nor respect for any human person. In the same town there was also a widow who kept on coming to him and saying, "Give me justice against my opponent!" For a long time he refused, but at last he said to himself, "Even though I have neither fear of God nor respect for any human person, I must grant this widow justice since she is such a nuisance, or in the end she will come and slap me in the face."'

And the Lord said, 'Do you hear what the unjust judge has to say? Now, will not God grant justice to his chosen ones who keep calling to him day and night even though he delays? I promise you, he will grant justice to them, and speedily. But when the Son of man comes, will he find faith on earth?'

Other readings: Exodus 17:8–13   Psalm 120 (121)   2 Timothy 3:14–4:2

THIS GOSPEL READING PRESENTS us with the stark choice facing us all. Are we people of faith who amid all the troubles of the world know that we are in the hands of God? Or are we faithless and despairing? When the Son of Man comes, will he indeed find faith on the earth?

The widow who prays for justice against her enemy reflects the plight of so many millions who cry out to God to put right the injustices of the world. The human yearning that the life of all people be respected and fostered is deeply felt by Christians.

Christians know that God has entrusted to creation, and to human beings, the awesome gift of freedom, which has both wonderful and devastating consequences. Freedom makes possible acts of selfless heroism, courage and generosity, the finest expressions of that human love which reflects the love of God. Freedom also makes possible acts of unutterable cruelty and hatred, which are equally the free choice of human beings.

The prayer of the widow represents the anguish of so many millions who cry out for justice and a resolution of the problems of the world. Amid such widespread distress Christians point to the overriding loving kindness of God, who 'will grant justice'. The reality of God's loving kindness is seen repeatedly in the loving human responses to the troubles of this world, and above all in the self-giving love of Christ, made present at each Eucharist.

Faith tells us that we are constantly held by God. It is crucial to confront the power of self-obsession and disbelief with the power of loving kindness, faith and prayer.

Do I trust in the overriding goodness of God amid all the troubles of the world?

Do I blame God for suffering and pain?

Let us pray for faith to inspire our words and deeds.

Let us ask for the gift of perseverance in prayer.

Thirtieth Sunday in Ordinary Time (Year C)

Luke 18:9–14

He spoke the following parable to some people who prided themselves on being righteous, and despised everyone else, 'Two men went up to the Temple to pray, one a Pharisee, the other a tax collector. The Pharisee stood there and said this prayer to himself, "I thank you, God, that I am not grasping, unjust, adulterous like everyone else, and particularly that I am not like this tax collector here. I fast twice a week; I pay tithes on all I possess." The tax collector stood at a distance, not daring even to raise his eyes to heaven; but he beat his breast and said, "God, be merciful to me, a sinner." This man, I tell you, went home again justified; the other did not. For everyone who raises himself up will be humbled, but anyone who humbles himself will be raised up.'

Other readings: Ecclesiasticus 35:12–14, 16–19   Psalm 33 (34) 2 Timothy 4:6–8, 16–18

THIS IS ANOTHER OF those wonderful parables which are only recorded in the Gospel of Luke. The parable of the Pharisee and the tax-collector, rather like the parable of the rich man and Lazarus, describes a stark contrast.

Jesus gives a caricature of a Pharisee who is inordinately proud of his achievements, one who completes all that the Law requires, and far more besides. Jesus describes the Pharisee as praying 'to himself'. This could simply mean that he was praying softly, but it seems also to suggest that the prayers of this man can never reach God. They are simply an expression of his pride and self-obsession, which is accompanied by a judgemental attitude to others.

We should be careful not to extend this negative portrayal of one Pharisees to all Pharisees, as has often been done in interpreting the gospels, for many members of this religious group were exemplary in their attitudes and conduct.

The tax-collector recognises his need of forgiveness. The gospels are full of references to tax-collectors, who were often dishonest, and sought the company of Jesus along with other 'sinners' (as in Luke 15:1). This man is deeply conscious of his need for God. He stands far off because he recognises that the God of holiness is to be found in the Temple, and he feels unworthy to come closer. He is a man of genuine faith and he beats his breast in an honest expression of his need.

'Justification', being 'at rights with God', is not a result of our own efforts to accumulate good deeds, but comes as a free gift to those who acknowledge their sinfulness and believe in the forgiveness Christ offers.

*Are my efforts to do good an attempt to win God over, or an
    expression of love for the God who forgives me?*
Do I pray as my heart directs me, or as I imagine I should?
Let us pray for those who are desperate to please God.
Let us pray for the faith which acknowledges the need of forgiveness.

Thirty-first Sunday in Ordinary Time
(Year C)

Luke 19:1–10

He entered Jericho and was going through the town and
suddenly a man whose name was Zacchaeus made his
appearance; he was a chief tax collector and a wealthy man.
He kept trying to see which Jesus was, but he was too short
and could not see him for the crowd; so he ran ahead and
climbed a sycamore tree to catch a glimpse of Jesus as he
was to pass that way. When Jesus reached the spot he looked
up and said to him, 'Zacchaeus, come down. Hurry, for
I am to stay at your house today.' And he hurried down
and welcomed him joyfully. When they saw that, they all
grumbled, saying that he had gone to stay at a sinner's house.
But Zacchaeus stood his ground and said to the Lord, 'Look,
Lord, I am giving half my property to the poor, and if I have
cheated anyone I will pay back four times the amount.' And
Jesus said to him, 'Today salvation has come to this house,
because he too is a son of Abraham; for the Son of man has
come to seek out and save what was lost.'

**Other readings: Wisdom 11:22–12:2 Psalm 144 (145)
2 Thessalonians 1:11–2:2**

THE STORY OF THE chief tax-collector Zacchaeus is of
considerable importance in the Gospel of Luke, for in it Jesus
declares that the purpose of his coming is 'to seek out and save what
was lost' (verse 10). Only Luke tells us about Zacchaeus. The harsh
criticism by the religious leaders of the welcome Jesus shows to
sinners becomes more widespread in this passage. Now everyone

is complaining: 'He has gone to stay at a sinner's house' (verse 7).

Zacchaeus is quite determined to meet Jesus, and allows no obstacle to get in his way. His climbing the sycamore tree illustrates that sometimes strenuous efforts are needed to rise above fears and preoccupations and to see the forgiving face of the Lord.

As it was in chapter 7 in the case of the woman who was a sinner, the encounter with Jesus is life-changing for Zacchaeus too. He realises that Jesus brings forgiveness. He decides to give away half his property and to make amends for what he has defrauded. Forgiveness can bring profound changes in a person's life. Zacchaeus now knows that he is no longer an isolated individual caught up in his own greed and selfishness, but truly a member of God's people. Jesus confirms this insight: 'He too is a son of Abraham' (verse 9).

The story comes just before the arrival of Jesus in Jerusalem. The final words of Jesus summarise both what he has shown in his ministry and what he will do in Jerusalem: 'The Son of Man has come to seek out and save what was lost.'

Do I recognise my need for forgiveness and the need to make changes in my life?
Do I allow the preoccupations of life to obscure my view of Jesus?
Let us pray for those who are approaching forgiveness and faith.
Let us pray for those who are critical of the free gift of forgiveness.

Thirty-second Sunday in Ordinary Time (Year C)

Luke 20:27–38

Some Sadducees – those who deny that there is a resurrection – approached him and they put this question to him, 'Teacher, Moses prescribed for us, *if a man's married brother dies childless, the man shall marry the widow to raise up children for his brother*. Well then, there were seven brothers; the first, having married a wife, died childless. The second and then the third married the widow. And the same with all seven, they died leaving no children. Finally the woman herself died. Now, at the resurrection, whose wife will she be, since she had been married to all seven?'

Jesus replied, 'The children of this world take wives and husbands, but those who are judged worthy of a place in that world and in the resurrection from the dead do not marry because they can no longer die, for they are the same as the angels, and being children of the resurrection they are children of God. And Moses himself implies that the dead rise again, in the passage about the bush, where he calls the Lord *the God of Abraham, the God of Isaac and the God of Jacob.* Now he is God, not of the dead, but of the living; for to him everyone is alive.'

Other readings: 2 Maccabees 7:1–2, 9–14   Psalm 16 (17)
2 Thessalonians 2:16–3:5

ONCE JESUS ARRIVES IN Jerusalem the three synoptic gospels (Mark, Matthew and Luke) give accounts of discussions and arguments that Jesus has with the religious leaders. These exchanges testify to the growing hostility of the Jewish leaders to Jesus. Our passage reports a discussion with the Sadducees, a group of Jews who did not believe in the resurrection of the dead.

Ideas about the after-life developed only slowly during Old Testament times, and received a significant boost at the time of the persecution of the Jewish faith in the second century BC and the subsequent Maccabean revolt. Our first reading narrates the martyrdom of seven brothers at this time and their strong faith in the resurrection.

Jesus is quick to point out that the life of the resurrection is quite different from earthly life. Above all, death will not bring this risen life to an end. He goes on to refute the position of the Sadducees in relation to the resurrection. They had sought justification from Moses. Jesus in his turn refers to the vision of the burning bush which Moses saw on Mount Horeb (Exodus 3). The God of Abraham, Isaac and Jacob is God of the living, the God of the resurrection, the God who raises human beings from death. That God is indeed the God of the resurrection will be demonstrated in the events that will now unfold in Jerusalem.

*Do I trust in the Christian hope that God's care and power go beyond
    death?*

Do I respect the life of every human being?

Let us pray for those who live without hope.

Let us pray for all our deceased brothers and sisters.

Thirty-third Sunday in Ordinary Time (Year C)

Luke 21:5–19

When some were talking about the Temple, remarking how it was adorned with fine stonework and votive offerings, he said, 'All these things you see – the time will come when not a single stone will be left on another which will not be pulled down.' And they put to him a question, saying, 'Teacher, when will this happen, and what sign will there be that it is about to take place?'

But he said, 'Take care not to be led astray, for many will come using my name and saying, "I am the one" and "The time is near at hand." Do not follow them. And when you hear of wars and upheavals, do not be terrified, for these things must happen first, but the end will not come at once.' Then he said to them, 'Nation will rise up against nation, and kingdom against kingdom. There will be great earthquakes and plagues and famines in various places; there will be terrifying events and great signs from heaven.

'But before all this happens, they will lay hands on you and persecute you, handing you over to the synagogues and prisons, and you will be brought before kings and governors for the sake of my name. This will give you opportunity to bear witness. Make up your minds not to prepare your defence in advance, for I myself shall give you an eloquence and a wisdom that none of your opponents will be able to resist or contradict. You will be betrayed even by parents and brothers, relations and friends; and they will put some of you to death. You will be hated by all on account of my name, but not a hair of your head will be lost. By your endurance you will win your lives.'

Other readings: Malachi 3:19–20   Psalm 97 (98)   2 Thessalonians 3:7–12

EACH OF THE SYNOPTIC gospels (Mark, Matthew and Luke) contains a report of the words of Jesus about the future and the end of the world. These words are pronounced by Jesus in Jerusalem shortly before his passion and death. The location is in the vicinity of the temple, and Jesus announces that one day it will be destroyed.

This topic leads into broader teachings about trust in God in the midst of disasters and persecutions. Christians are not to waste time calculating when the end will come. They are not to allow themselves to be misled by false prophets and false messiahs. Above all, they are to trust in the provident care of God, who will give them eloquence and wisdom to defend themselves and preach the truth. 'By your endurance you will win your lives.'

Am I fearful about the future or do I trust in the providence of God?
Do I waste my energy calculating how to reach salvation?
We pray for all victims of natural disasters and religious persecution.
We pray for the gift of patient endurance.

Christ the King (Year C)

Luke 23:35–43

The people stood watching. As for the leaders, they scoffed at him saying, 'He saved others, let him save himself if he is the Messiah of God, the Chosen One.' The soldiers mocked him too, coming up to him, offering him vinegar, and saying, 'If you are the king of the Jews, save yourself.' There was also an inscription over him: 'This is the King of the Jews'.

One of the criminals hanging there jeered at him: 'Are you not the Messiah? Save yourself and us.' But in reply the other rebuked him saying. 'Do you not fear God, since you are under the same sentence? And we justly, for we are getting what we deserve for what we did. But this man did nothing wrong.' Then he said, 'Jesus, remember me when you come into your kingdom.' He answered him, 'Amen I say to you, today you will be with me in paradise.'

Other readings: 2 Samuel 5:1–3 Psalm 121 (122) Colossians 1:12–20

IT MIGHT SEEM STRANGE that this part of the story of Christ's passion and death is read on the feast of Christ the King. How is it that this gospel reading was chosen?

The debate about whether Jesus is properly called the anointed king or Messiah takes us to the heart of the drama of the gospel. The leaders taunt Jesus: 'let him save himself if he is the Christ of God'. The soldiers mock Jesus for claiming to be 'the king of the Jews'. The truth is proclaimed somewhat ironically by the inscription on the cross. But Jesus did not come to win a worldly kingdom, and throughout his public ministry he was wary of any messianic claims made for him.

It is in the dialogue with the 'good thief', the criminal crucified with him who is well disposed towards him, that we come to know the truth about the kingdom of Jesus. His kingdom is not of this world. It is the kingdom of God, where peace and mercy reign, not an earthly kingdom which can be fought over in war and violence.

The heart of the message of this gospel is that Jesus welcomes the repentant sinner, no matter how grievous his offence, into the kingdom, into the arms of the loving Father. This is an appropriate passage with which to end our Sunday-by-Sunday reading of the Gospel of Luke. Jesus has come to 'bring good news to the poor' (4:18), and to 'seek out and save the lost' (19:10). Those who turn to Jesus come into his company in the kingdom of God.

Have I understood the good news preached by Jesus in the Gospel of Luke?

What will stay with me particularly from the Gospel of Luke?

Let us pray for perseverance as we journey towards God's kingdom of love and peace.

Jesus, remember me when you come into your kingdom.

SOLEMNITIES AND FEASTS OF THE LORD

Feast of the Presentation of the Lord

Luke 2:22–40

And when the days were complete for them to be purified in keeping with the Law of Moses, they took him up to Jerusalem to present him to the Lord – as it is written in the Law of the Lord: *Every first-born male shall be called holy to the Lord* – and also to offer in sacrifice, in accordance with what is prescribed in the Law of the Lord, *a pair of turtledoves or two young pigeons.* Now in Jerusalem there was a man named Simeon. He was a righteous and devout man, looking forward to the consolation of Israel, and the Holy Spirit rested on him. It had been revealed to him by the Holy Spirit that he would not see death until he had seen the Christ of the Lord. Prompted by the Spirit he came into the Temple; and when the parents brought in the child Jesus to do for him what the Law required, Simeon himself took him into his arms and blessed God and said:

> Now, Master, you are letting your servant
> go in peace according to your word;
> for my eyes have seen your salvation
> which you have made ready in the presence of all nations;
> a light for revelation to the gentiles
> and for the glory of your people Israel.

As the child's father and mother were wondering at the things that were being said about him, Simeon blessed them and said to Mary his mother, 'Look, he is destined for the fall and for the rise of many in Israel, destined to be a sign that is opposed – and a sword will pierce your soul too – so that the thoughts of many may be laid bare.'

There was a prophetess, too, Anna the daughter of Phanuel, of the tribe of Asher. She was advanced in years, having lived with her husband seven years after her marriage, then as a widow to the age of eighty-four. She never left the Temple, worshipping night and day with fasting and prayer. She came up just at that moment and began to praise God; and to speak about the child to all who looked forward to the deliverance of Jerusalem.

When they had completed everything according to the Law of the Lord, they went back to Galilee, to their own town of Nazareth. And the child grew and became strong, filled with wisdom, and God's favour was on him.

Other readings: Malachi 3:1–4   Psalm 23 (24)   Hebrews 2:14–18

THIS LENGTHY GOSPEL READING completes for us the mystery of Christmas. Jesus becomes 'completely like his brothers'. He is brought to the Temple to begin a life of service. His future path is foreseen by Simeon and Anna. His mother's pain is also foretold. He is subject to his parents in the secret life of Nazareth. But, as Simeon already proclaims, he is set to be a 'sign that is opposed', 'a light for revelation to the gentiles and for the glory of his people Israel'.

How does this feast reconnect us with the Christmas mysteries?
What deeper significance does Jesus' coming to the Temple contain?
Consider on this feast of Candlemas how light is a recurring theme in Bible and liturgy.
We pray for all fathers and mothers that they may treasure their children as gifts of God.

Trinity Sunday (Year A)

John 3:16–18
Jesus said to Nicodemus:

'For God loved the world so much
that he gave his only-begotten Son,
so that everyone who believes in him
may not perish but may have eternal life.
For God sent his Son into the world

not to judge the world,
but so that the world might be saved through him.
One who believes in him will not be judged;
but whoever does not believe is judged already,
for not believing in the name of God's only-begotten Son.'

Other readings: Exodus 34:4–6, 8–9 Daniel 3:52–56 2 Corinthians 13:11–13

THE EASTER SEASON HAS come to an end, and we might have
expected that the Sunday after Pentecost would be simply one of
those Sundays of the year 'in ordinary time'. The Solemnity of the
Most Holy Trinity, Trinity Sunday, gives us the opportunity to reflect
on the mystery of God, the God who has been revealed to us above
all in the death and resurrection of Jesus, the Son of God, and in the
outpouring of the Holy Spirit.

In our gospel reading Jesus teaches Nicodemus, who is searching
for the truth, about the basic motivation of God in sending us the
only Son. This motivation is love. In creating us God also makes it
possible for us to accept the love of God with complete freedom,
for we can refuse this love. Believing in 'the name of God's only-
begotten Son' means acknowledging the reality of the love of God
for each of us. We are challenged to allow the love of God into our
lives again and again in the daily decisions we must make to embrace
what is good and to shun what is evil. If we reject goodness, it is not
God who condemns us. We condemn ourselves.

The essence of God's attitude towards human beings is clear already
in the first reading from the Book of Exodus, when the Lord is revealed
as a 'God of tenderness and compassion, slow to anger, and rich in
kindness and faithfulness'. These qualities of God are illustrated as the
story of salvation progresses and most fully when, in the fulness of time,
God sends the incarnate Son to live and die for us, and pours out the
Holy Spirit to be the constant presence of God's love in the world.

St Paul's final greeting to the people of Corinth in the second reading
sums up our prayer on this feast: 'The grace of the Lord Jesus Christ, the
love of God and the fellowship of the Holy Spirit be with you all.'

Have I accepted in my heart that God is 'a God of compassion'?
*Do I understand that faith is essentially trusting in God who loves and
    saves me?*

Pray for a renewed sense of the awesomeness of God.
Pray for those who struggle with the notion of a God who loves them.

Trinity Sunday (Year B)

Matthew 28:16–20

Now the eleven disciples set out for Galilee, to the mountain to which Jesus had directed them. When they saw him they worshipped him, though some hesitated. Jesus came up and spoke to them. He said, 'All authority in heaven and on earth has been given to me. Go, therefore, make disciples of all nations; baptise them in the name of the Father and of the Son and of the Holy Spirit, and teach them to observe everything I have commanded you. And look, I am with you always till the end of time.'

Other readings: Deuteronomy 4:32–34, 39–40 Psalm 32 (33)
Romans 8:14–17

THE GOSPEL OF MATTHEW ends with this passage. This is the commission which the Risen Jesus gives to his disciples. In it there is reference to baptism 'in the name of the Father, and of the Son and of the Holy Spirit'.

The doctrine of the Holy Trinity is the fruit of a long process of learning and understanding as the revelation of God as Father, Son and Holy Spirit is received by human minds and put into human words. In Old Testament times, as our reading from the Book of Deuteronomy indicates, the people were aware that God was close to them, protected them and gave them the law. Unlike the gods of the nations, the God of Moses became involved with the people and was concerned for them.

The books of the Old Testament also witness to a growing awareness of the Spirit of God. This Spirit gave strength to people and inspired the prophets to speak the word, a word sometimes of judgement, but often of encouragement and consolation.

Jesus, the Son of God, is the fulness of revelation. He is the Word of God for us. By his death and resurrection he shows that God is with us to free us from sin and death. Jesus speaks of his bond with the Father, and is keenly aware of the power of the Spirit. It did not take long for Christians to acknowledge that God is Father, Son and Holy Spirit, and in time we see the emergence of the doctrine of the Holy Trinity, of three 'persons' in one God.

One week after the end of the Easter season, in which we gave thanks for the saving death and resurrection of Jesus, and the celebration of the gift of the Holy Spirit on Pentecost Sunday, this feast of the Holy Trinity invites us to contemplate the mystery of God to the extent that our minds are able. Paul in the Letter to the Romans reminds us that the Spirit of God makes us God's children, destined to share in the life of God, as Christ does. Through the Holy Spirit dwelling in our hearts we become aware of the love and strength of the living God available to us both now and in the life to come.

What does it mean to me that God is Father, Son and Holy Spirit?
Do I dismiss the doctrine of the Holy Trinity as a conundrum which
*   is difficult to grasp?*
Pray for a deeper awareness of the love of God demonstrated in the Trinity.
Pray for those who consider the mystery of God to be a delusion.

Trinity Sunday (Year C)

John 16:12–15
Jesus said:

> 'I still have many things to say to you
> but you cannot bear them now.
> However, when the Spirit of truth comes
> he will guide you in all truth,
> since he will not be speaking on his own account,
> but will say only what he has been told;
> and he will reveal to you the things to come.
> He will glorify me,
> since he will take what is mine and reveal it to you.
> Everything the Father has is mine;
> that is why I said
> he will take what is mine and reveal it to you.'

Other readings: Proverbs 8:22–31 Psalm 8 Romans 5:1–5

EVEN THOUGH WE CAME to the end of the Easter season with the feast of Pentecost, the atmosphere of celebration continues this Sunday with Trinity Sunday. After the long seasons of Lent and Easter it is as if we pause to contemplate the mystery of God, the mystery of the Three in One, the mystery of the Holy Trinity.

The gospel reading allows us to reflect on this mystery, for Father, Son and Spirit are clearly present in it. The passage is taken from the farewell speeches in the Gospel of John, from which we have read during the Easter season. Jesus is about to leave his disciples to return to the Father.

The Spirit of truth, referred to earlier in John's gospel as the 'Advocate', the one 'called to be alongside', will lead the disciples further into the fulness of truth. The presence of the Spirit in the Church allows us to discover new things, new depths which are implicit in the good news of Jesus, but which only with time become clear to us. The Spirit is the guarantor that the Church remains in the truth.

The unity of Father, Son and Spirit is underlined when Jesus says that all that the Spirit speaks will be from him, and all that is from him is from the Father. We are confronted with the beauty of the God who reaches out to us, and the deep mystery of God, which is beyond our capacity to explain.

As St Paul makes clear in the passage from Romans, it is through the reaching out of Jesus Christ that we are at peace with God, and through the outpouring of the Holy Spirit that we know our hope in God is sound.

Consider how each of the persons of the Holy Trinity reaches out to us.
What do I need to do to allow the Spirit to lead me 'to the complete truth'?
Pray for reverence and humility when faced with the mystery of the one, true God.
Pray for those who seek the truth but cannot open their hearts to it.

The Body and Blood of Christ (Year A)

John 6:51–58
Jesus said:

'I am the living bread which has come down from heaven.
Anyone who eats of this bread will live for ever;
and the bread that I shall give
is my flesh, for the life of the world.'

Then the Jews started arguing among themselves, 'How can this man give us his flesh to eat?'

So Jesus said to them:

'Amen, Amen I say to you,
if you do not eat the flesh of the Son of man
and drink his blood,
you have no life in you.
Anyone who does eat my flesh
and drink my blood has eternal life,
and I shall raise up that person on the last day.
For my flesh is true food
and my blood is true drink.
Whoever eats my flesh and drinks my blood
dwells in me
and I dwell in that person.
As the living Father sent me
and I live through the Father,
so whoever eats me will also live through me.
This is the bread which came down from heaven;
not like the bread our ancestors ate and died.
Anyone who eats this bread will live for ever.'

Other readings: Deuteronomy 8:2–3, 14–16 Psalm 147 1 Corinthians 10:16–17

THE SOLEMNITY OF THE Body and Blood of the Lord, which we know also as Corpus Christi, provides a special occasion to consider the gift of the Holy Eucharist, the gift given by Christ to the Church on the night before he died.

The gospel is taken from chapter 6 of the Fourth Gospel, a lengthy chapter which presents the multiplication of the loaves and the walking on the water, followed by the words of Jesus and interventions of the Jews concerning the meaning of the first of these two signs. The verses in today's reading come towards the end of the chapter, when the words of Jesus clearly focus on the Eucharist.

In the Eucharist we receive repeatedly the once-and-for-all gift of the Bread of Life. As Jesus implies, it is unlike anything which preceded it, unlike 'the bread our ancestors ate'. This bread is the pledge of God's gift of life, and is best understood in the context of the paschal mystery, the death of Christ and his self-giving to lead us to life.

Perhaps this feast may also be an occasion for us to question ourselves about the reverence we show to the Eucharist. The Church encourages us to prepare by prayer to receive both Word and Sacrament, to observe a one-hour fast before Communion (except for those who are infirm), to approach the table of the Lord reverently, to spend time in giving thanks for this extraordinary sacrament, and to show a particular respect and devotion to the Blessed Sacrament reserved in our churches.

How can you avoid receiving the Lord in a routine manner?
What can you do to increase your reverence for the Blessed Sacrament?
Pray that we will allow the reception of the Eucharist to transform our lives.
Pray for fidelity to our Sunday Mass obligation, that all may be strengthened in communion.

The Body and Blood of Christ (Year B)

Mark 14:12–16, 22–26

On the first day of Unleavened Bread, when they used to sacrifice the Passover lamb, his disciples said to him, 'Where do you want us to go and make the preparations for you to eat the Passover?' So he sent two of his disciples, saying to them, 'Go into the city and someone will meet you carrying a pitcher of water. Follow him, and wherever he enters say to the owner of the house, "The teacher says: Where is the room where I may eat the Passover with my disciples?" He will show you a large upper room ready set out. Make the preparations for us there.' The disciples set out and went to the city and found everything as he had told them, and prepared the Passover.

And as they were eating he took bread, and when he had said the blessing he broke it, gave it to them and said, 'Take it, this is my body.' Then taking a cup, after giving thanks he gave it to them, and all drank from it, and he said to them, 'This is my blood of the covenant, poured out for many. Amen I say to you, I shall never again drink wine until that day when I drink new wine in the kingdom of God.'

Having sung the psalms they left for the Mount of Olives.

Other readings: Exodus 24:3–8 Psalm 115 (116) Hebrews 9:11–15

THE SOLEMNITY OF THE Body and Blood of Christ is an opportunity to revisit the events of Holy Thursday, and in particular the institution of the Eucharist. It is against the background of Jesus' approaching death that we gain a deeper understanding of the actions of Jesus at the Last Supper.

The disciples are told to prepare the Passover. While the Jewish Passover feast celebrated God's goodness in liberating the chosen people from slavery in Egypt, the Supper that Jesus gives will commemorate the selfless love of his death on the cross, by which we are liberated and born to new life.

In blessing and sharing the bread and wine Jesus is giving himself. By doing this in memory of him his disciples make present through the centuries the gift and sacrifice of Jesus Christ. The Letter to the Hebrews illustrates how the death of Christ is the once-and-for-all sacrifice of himself for our salvation. It makes redundant all the sacrifices of the old law. It is by his own blood that Christ purifies us. The blood of goats and bulls is no longer necessary. This is why Christ's sacrifice is the sacrifice of the 'new covenant' of which we are the beneficiaries.

What does the Eucharist mean to me?
How can I avoid a sense of routine as I take part in the Mass?
Pray for a deeper awareness of being drawn into the Body of
*   Christ by receiving the Eucharist.*
Pray for a sense of unity with God's people as we share 'one
*   bread' and 'one cup'.*

The Body and Blood of Christ (Year C)

Luke 9:11–17

But the crowds got to know and followed him. He made them welcome and talked to them about the kingdom of God; and he cured those who were in need of healing.

The day was tending towards evening when the Twelve came up to him and said, 'Send the crowd away, so that they can go to the villages and farms round about to find lodging and food; for we are in a deserted place here.' He replied, 'Give them something to eat yourselves.' But they said, 'We have no more than five loaves and two fish, unless we are to go ourselves and buy food for all these people.' For there were about five thousand men. But he said to his disciples, 'Get them to sit down in parties of about fifty.' They did so and got them all to sit down. Then taking the five loaves and the two fish, and raising his eyes to heaven, he blessed them and broke them and began handing them to his disciples to set before the crowd. They all ate as much as they wanted, and what was left over from them was taken up, twelve baskets of broken pieces.

Other readings: Genesis 14:18–20   Psalm 109 (110)   1 Corinthians 11:23–26

THE SOLEMNITY OF THE Body and Blood of the Lord, which we know also as Corpus Christi, gives us an opportunity to revisit the events of Holy Thursday. That day was full of material to ponder, and, now that Lent and Easter are complete, this feast provides an opportunity for deeper reflection on the mystery of the Eucharist instituted by Christ on the night before he died.

Jesus acknowledges the need of the crowd and shows compassion for them. He 'makes them welcome', speaks to them about the Kingdom of God, and heals the sick. This attitude of Jesus contrasts with that of the Twelve, who are insistent that the crowds be sent away. Jesus' reply to this is: 'Give them something to eat yourselves.' The Christian, like Jesus, must recognise the needs, both material and spiritual, of those who are searching for the Kingdom.

The narrative of the miracle itself, especially in the detail of the actions of Jesus in verse 16, clearly prepares for the Last Supper. The miracle of the loaves, then, does not only look back to God's past provision for the people, such as the provision of manna in the desert, but also points to the Eucharist and to the self-giving of Christ on the cross.

St Paul reminds us explicitly of what Jesus did 'on the night that he was betrayed'. He gives us not an earthly bread, but the bread which is the gift of himself that we might live.

How can we conform our lives to the self-giving of Christ in the Eucharist?
What might Jesus' words to 'give them something to eat yourselves'
suggest to us today?
Pray for true reverence for the gift of Christ's Body and Blood in the
Eucharist.
Pray for a deeper understanding that it is the Eucharist which makes
the Church.

The Birth of John the Baptist

Luke 1:57–66, 80

The time came for Elizabeth to give birth, and she gave birth to a son; and her neighbours and relations heard that the Lord had lavished his mercy on her, and they shared her joy.

Now it happened that on the eighth day they came to circumcise the child; they were going to call him Zechariah after his father, but his mother spoke up, saying, 'No, he shall be called John.' They said to her, 'But no one in your family has that name,' and made signs to his father to find out what he wanted him called. The father asked for a writing-tablet and wrote, 'His name is John.' And they were all astonished. Immediately his mouth was opened and his tongue freed and he began to speak praising God. Fear came over all their neighbours, and the whole affair was talked about throughout the hill country of Judaea. All those who heard of it took it to heart, saying, 'What then is this child to be?' And indeed the hand of the Lord was with him.

And the child grew and was strengthened in spirit. And he lived in the desert until the day he appeared openly to Israel.

Other readings: Isaiah 49:1–6 Psalm 138 (139) Acts 13:22–26

THE SOLEMNITY OF THE Birth of John the Baptist takes precedence over the ordinary Sunday which we would otherwise be celebrating. The birth of the one who prepares the way for Christ is a most significant landmark in the history of salvation.

In the first two chapters of Luke's gospel the births of John the Baptist and of Jesus are recounted. The birth of John, from elderly parents, is an extraordinary gift of God, but will be overshadowed by the birth of Jesus, conceived in the womb of the Virgin Mary. Luke stresses the joy which accompanies these births.

On the day of circumcision and naming extraordinary events occur. Both his mother and his father know that he is to be called 'John', which means 'God is compassionate.' John's father, Zechariah, loses his temporary dumbness once he has confirmed Elizabeth's insight that this child will be the herald of God's loving mercy.

The people sense something extraordinary is happening. 'What then is this child to be?' As the gospel story unfolds, John the Baptist is shown to be the herald and baptiser of the Messiah and a great preacher of the truth. The Preface from today's feast celebrates him as 'chosen from all the prophets to show the world its redeemer' and as 'found worthy of a martyr's death, his last and greatest act of witness'.

How does John's name encapsulate his mission?

Recall the different features of John's unique role in the history of salvation.

Pray for a deeper acceptance of the gift of salvation heralded by John the Baptist.

Pray for the strength to imitate John's fidelity to the truth.

Solemnity of Saints Peter and Paul

Matthew 16:13–19

When Jesus came to the region of Caesarea Philippi he put this question to his disciples, 'Who do people say the Son of man is?' And they said, 'Some say John the Baptist, some Elijah, and others Jeremiah or one of the prophets.' He said to them, 'But you, who do you say I am?' In answer Simon Peter said, 'You are the Messiah, the Son of the living God.' In reply Jesus said to him, 'Blessed are you, Simon son of Jonah, for flesh and blood has not revealed this to you but my Father in heaven. So I now say to you: "You are Peter and on this rock I will build my church. And the gates of the underworld will never overpower it. I will give you the keys of the kingdom of Heaven: whatever you bind on earth will be bound in heaven; whatever you loose on earth will be loosed in heaven."'

Other readings: Acts 12:1–11   Psalm 33 (34)   2 Timothy 4:6–8, 17–18

ON THIS DAY WE celebrate the feast of the two great apostles, Peter and Paul. One was with Jesus from the beginning of his ministry and accompanied him until the end. His faith was sorely tested by seeing his Messiah suffer. The life of the other was dramatically changed by an encounter with the Risen Jesus. From persecuting Christians he became a preacher of the faith.

The gospels provide many stories about St Peter, which might have been chosen for today's feast. The reading from the Gospel of Matthew tells of Peter's faith in Jesus as the Messiah. His declaration of faith leads to his commissioning by Jesus. Despite the trials he will face, Peter's faith endures.

Our second reading reminds us that St Paul spent his life travelling and proclaiming the gospel beyond the confines of Judaism. He 'fought the good fight' to the end. While Peter is commonly recalled as the one who preached to the people of Israel, Paul is revered as the 'apostle of the gentiles'. In fact both of them preached to both Jew and Gentile.

On this feast we are invited to consider the life and teaching of St Paul, and above all his letters preserved in the New Testament. The heart of Paul's message, the heart of his gospel, is that we are saved by our faith in Christ. This faith was already expressed by Peter as he accompanied Jesus in his ministry. The same faith is what Paul came to know by a 'revelation' of the Risen Jesus. Christ's disciples today have come to know the good news because people like Peter and Paul were brave enough to give their lives for it and to proclaim it to the whole world.

What does the faith of Peter in the gospel reading teach me?
How does the faithful witness of Paul inspire me to spread the good news?

We thank God for all the martyrs who gave, and still give, their lives
   for the gospel.
We pray for those who have lost sight of Jesus amid the problems and
   distractions of life.

The Transfiguration of the Lord

Year A: Matthew 17:1–9

Six days later, Jesus took with him Peter and James and his brother John and led them up a high mountain on their own. In their presence he was transfigured: his face shone like the sun and his clothes became as dazzling as light. And suddenly Moses and Elijah appeared to them, talking with him. Then Peter spoke to Jesus, saying, 'Lord, it is wonderful for us to be here; if you want me to, I will make three shelters here, one for you, one for Moses and one for Elijah.' He was still speaking when suddenly a bright cloud covered them with shadow, and suddenly from the cloud there came a voice which said, 'This is my Son, the Beloved; he enjoys my favour. Listen to him.' When they heard this, the disciples fell on their faces, overcome with fear. But Jesus came up and touched them, saying, 'Stand up, do not be afraid.' And when they raised their eyes they saw no one but Jesus himself alone.

As they came down from the mountain Jesus gave them this order, 'Tell no one about this vision until the Son of man has risen from the dead.'

Year B: Mark 9:2–10

Six days later, Jesus took with him Peter and James and John and led them up a high mountain on their own by themselves. In their presence he was transfigured: his clothes became brilliantly white, whiter than any earthly bleacher could make them. Elijah appeared to them with Moses; and they were talking to Jesus. Then Peter spoke to Jesus, 'Rabbi,' he said, 'it is wonderful for us to be here; so let us make three shelters, one for you, one for Moses and one for Elijah.' He did not know what to say; they were so frightened. And a cloud came, covering them in shadow; and from the cloud came a voice, 'This is my Son, the Beloved. Listen to him.' Then suddenly, when they looked round, they saw no one with them any more but only Jesus.

As they were coming down from the mountain he instructed them to tell no one what they had seen, except when the Son of man had risen from the dead. And they kept the matter to themselves, though they puzzled what 'rising from the dead' could mean.

Year C: Luke 9:28–36

Now about eight days after these sayings, taking Peter, John and James with him he went up the mountain to pray. And it happened that, as he was praying, the aspect of his face was changed and his clothing became dazzling white. And suddenly there were two men talking to him; they were Moses and Elijah appearing in glory, and they were speaking of his departure which he was to accomplish in Jerusalem. Peter and his companions were heavy with sleep, but when they were fully awake they saw his glory and the two men standing with him. As these were leaving him, Peter said to Jesus, 'Master, it is wonderful for us to be here; so let us make three shelters, one for you, one for Moses and one for Elijah,' not knowing what he was saying. While he was saying this, a cloud came and covered them with shadow; and as they went into the cloud the disciples were afraid. And a voice came from the cloud saying, 'This is my Son, the Chosen One. Listen to him.' And after the voice had spoken, Jesus was found alone. They themselves kept silence and, in those days, told no one what they had seen.

Other readings: Daniel 7:9–10, 13–14 Psalm 96 (97) 2 Peter 1:16–19

SINCE IT IS A FEAST of the Lord, the Transfiguration takes precedence over the ordinary Sunday celebration whenever 6th August falls on a Sunday. The Gospel of the Transfiguration is read, as it is every year on the Second Sunday of Lent, when we recall the journey of Jesus to Jerusalem.

In the Gospels of Matthew, Mark and Luke, all of whom recount the incident, it is found just as Jesus is beginning his journey to Jerusalem, where he will be arrested, tortured and executed. The

Transfiguration provides a glimpse of something beyond the apparent tragedy of the Cross. Jesus is at prayer and it is at this moment that the disciples witness a transformation. Both his face and his garments are miraculously changed, suggesting something beyond our experience.

The vision seen by the three disciples is further enriched by the presence of Moses and Elijah, who can be understood as bearing witness to Jesus. It is they who along with so many prophets and holy people have prepared for the coming of the Messiah.

The cloud and the voice are also part of this experience. As on so many occasions in the Old Testament they speak of the presence of God. The climax comes when God speaks, calling Jesus his 'beloved Son', and commanding the disciples to 'listen'.

As Jesus makes his way to Jerusalem, courageously facing whatever will meet him there, the disciples are encouraged to follow his way. They may well face suffering and even death, but the way of Jesus truly leads to life. The event so struck the three disciples that they never forgot it, and it became a valuable part of the gospel witness to Jesus, assuring all faithful disciples of future glory.

Why do we celebrate the Transfiguration of Jesus?
What is the sense of the presence of Moses and Elijah?
*We thank God for the faithful witness of Christ, who encourages us
    on our journey.*
*We pray for a deeper appreciation of the witness of the prophets and
    evangelists.*

The Assumption of Our Lady

Luke 1:39–56

Mary set out at that time and went with haste into the hill country to a town in Judah. She went into Zechariah's house and greeted Elizabeth. Now it happened that when Elizabeth heard Mary's greeting, the child leapt in her womb and Elizabeth was filled with the Holy Spirit. She gave a loud cry and said, 'Blessed are you among women, and blessed is the fruit of your womb. Why has this happened to me, that the mother of my Lord should come to me? Look, as soon as your greeting reached my ears, the child in my womb leapt for joy. And, blessed is she who believed that what was said to her from the Lord would be fulfilled.'

And Mary said:

'My soul proclaims the greatness of the Lord
and my spirit *rejoices in God my Saviour*;
since *he has looked with favour on the lowliness of his servant.*
For see, from now on all generations will call me blessed,
for the Almighty has done great things for me,
and *holy is his name*,
and *his mercy is from generation to generation on those
    who fear him.*
He has exerted the power of his arm,
he has scattered the proud in the thoughts of their heart.
He has taken down princes from thrones *and raised up
    the lowly.*
He has filled the hungry with good things, and sent the rich
    away empty.
He has come to the help of Israel his servant,
in remembrance of his mercy,
according to the promise he made to our ancestors,
of his mercy to Abraham and his descendants for ever.'

Mary stayed with her some three months and then went back home.

Other readings: Apocalypse 11:19 12:1–6, 10 Psalm 44 (45)
1 Corinthians 15:20–26

THERE IS OF COURSE no gospel reading which narrates the Assumption into heaven of the Blessed Virgin Mary, her sharing body and soul in the risen life of her Son. St Paul, in the second reading for the feast, speaks of Christ as the 'first-fruits' from the dead, and then of 'those who belong to him', who follow him into life. We can consider Mary to be the first among these, for she was the first to respond to the call to serve Christ.

The gospel reading demonstrates with what faith and generosity she answered God's call. She visits her cousin Elizabeth, filled with a spirit of prayer and praise, which is spelled out at length in her song of joy, the *Magnificat*. God's mercy to Abraham and his descendants, of which she sings, is a fidelity which never ends and which leads God's faithful people, body and soul, into the life of God.

The inexpressible glory of the risen life bestowed on Mary is suggested in the vision of the woman 'adorned with the sun, standing on the moon, and with twelve stars on her head' from the Book of Revelation, which has traditionally been used to celebrate the glory Mary receives through her being 'assumed' body and soul into the presence of God.

What does the feast of the Assumption tell us about the value of our bodies?
Why is it that Mary is so privileged by God?
We pray that we may be filled with the hope of the resurrection.
Let us pray for a deeper appreciation and love for the mother of Jesus.

Feast of the Exaltation of the Cross

John 3:13–17
Jesus said to Nicodemus:

> 'No one has ascended to heaven
> except the one who descended from heaven, the Son of man.
> As Moses lifted up the snake in the desert,
> so must the Son of man be lifted up
> so that everyone who believes in him
> may have eternal life.
> For God loved the world so much
> that he gave his only-begotten Son,
> so that everyone who believes in him
> may not perish but may have eternal life.
> For God sent his Son into the world
> not to judge the world,
> but so that the world might be saved through him.'

Other readings: Numbers 21:4–9   Psalm 77 (78)   Philippians 2:6–11
THE FEAST OF THE Exaltation of the Holy Cross takes precedence

over the ordinary Sunday Mass because it is a feast of the Lord. Bringing together the cross and 'exaltation' suggests immediately that the focus is on the paschal mystery of the death and resurrection of the Lord. It is true that this is the focus of every Mass. This feast originated in Jerusalem with the discovery of the true cross and the dedication of the Church of the Holy Sepulchre.

The writings of the New Testament help us to consider the true meaning of the death and resurrection of Jesus. The gospel for this feast is taken from the words of Jesus to Nicodemus in the third chapter of the Gospel of John. Jesus has been speaking about being 'born from above', the new birth through water and the Holy Spirit which Christians receive in baptism. This new birth, this new life, comes from the saving work of Jesus.

Jesus alludes to the lifting up of the serpent in the desert, which is narrated in the first reading from the Book of Numbers, in reference to his own being raised up on the cross. The final statements in the gospel passage are of extraordinary significance. The coming of the Son reveals the Father's love. The Son comes not to condemn but to offer life to the world.

The cross, the traditional instrument of torture and death in the Roman empire, is transformed into the symbol of new life, the life shared by Jesus with all those who believe. It is therefore logical that the cross becomes a symbol of triumph and exaltation. How strange it would be otherwise for Christians to 'cross themselves'!

St Paul recalls in the Letter to the Philippians the example of humility given by Christ for all to follow. His self-emptying in becoming man and in accepting death on the cross leads to the new life of the resurrection.

How can a symbol of torture and death become a sign of life?
What do I need to be able to carry the cross I have been asked to bear?
Let us thank God for the love shown in the death and resurrection of Jesus.
Let us pray for a true understanding of the paschal mystery in our own lives.

The Solemnity of All Saints

Matthew 5:1–12

Seeing the crowds, he went onto the mountain. And when he was seated his disciples came to him. Then he began to speak. This is what he taught them:

'Blessed are the poor in spirit, for the kingdom of Heaven is theirs.

Blessed are the gentle, for they shall inherit the earth.

Blessed are those who mourn, for they shall be comforted.

Blessed are those who hunger and thirst for righteousness, for they shall be filled.

Blessed are the merciful, for they shall receive mercy.

Blessed are the pure in heart, for they shall see God.

Blessed are the peacemakers, for they shall be called children of God.

Blessed are those who are persecuted in the cause of righteousness, for the kingdom of Heaven is theirs.

'Blessed are you when people abuse you and persecute you and speak all kinds of evil against you falsely on my account. Rejoice and be glad, for your reward will be great in heaven; this is how they persecuted the prophets before you.'

Other readings: Apocalypse 7:2–4, 9–14   Psalm 23 (24)   1 John 3:1–3

THE FEAST OF ALL Saints gathers together in one great celebration all those who throughout history have sought for God and found God in Christ. We celebrate our belonging to the great 'communion of saints' and long to be fully united with those who have gone before us 'marked with the sign of faith'. Should not our celebration include all those who in seeking what is true and good have searched for the one, true God?

Our gospel contains the opening words of the Sermon on the Mount. In these 'beatitudes' Jesus teaches us about the values, attitudes and actions of those who truly seek God. They do not seek their own advantage. Jesus promises the rewards of the kingdom for those who live in this way.

We are born into the life of the saints, of God's holy people, through our baptism and faith in Christ. But our other two readings for this feast look forward to the future life of the saints. John reminds us in the second reading that we can have no idea what our future will be like. But, he says, 'we shall be like him'. Christians are assured that they will be brought into the very life of God.

The book of the Apocalypse, or of Revelation, with its colourful visions of the future, is perhaps best suited to help us yearn for the life of God. It shows us that this life is for the present beyond our imagining. We know of it only through visions and images. In the vision depicted here we see those who have 'been through the great persecution'. We are reminded that so many of those who follow Christ in our day still give their lives in martyrdom. That way of following Christ may not be asked of us, but self-giving after the example of Christ is.

Do I treasure my membership of the Church, the holy people of God?
Do I try to make real in my life the simplicity of the beatitudes?
We celebrate being one with our brothers and sisters in the communion
*   of saints.*
We pray for all the faithful departed that they may have the fulness of life.

The Dedication of the Lateran Basilica

John 2:13–22

The time of the Jewish Passover was near and Jesus went up to Jerusalem. In the Temple he found people selling cattle and sheep and doves, and the money-changers sitting there. Making a whip out of cords, he began to drive them all out of the Temple, both sheep and cattle, scattered the money-changers' coins, overturned their tables and said to the dove-sellers, 'Take all this away from here and stop making my Father's house a market-house.' Then his disciples remembered that it had been written, *I am eaten up with zeal for your house.* The Jews in reply said, 'What sign can you show us for doing this?' Jesus answered, 'Destroy this Temple, and in three days I will raise it up.' The Jews replied, 'It took forty-six years to build this Temple: are you going to raise it up in three days?' But he was speaking about the Temple that was his body. When he had been raised from the dead, his disciples remembered that he had said this, and they believed the scripture and the words that he had spoken.

Other readings: Ezekiel 47:1–2, 8–9, 12   Psalm 45 (46)
1 Corinthians 3:9–11, 16–17

It may come as a surprise that the celebration of the dedication of the Lateran Basilica in Rome displaces the usual Sunday celebration. There are two reasons for this: the basilica's primary dedication is to the Saviour, and, being the cathedral of Rome, it is the mother church of the Christian world and takes precedence even over St Peter's in the Vatican.

The basilica of 'St John Lateran', as it is also called, since it is dedicated also to St John the Baptist, was built in the fourth century by the Roman emperor Constantine. It became the church of the bishop of Rome. For many centuries the popes lived at the Lateran. Close by is the baptistry where Constantine was baptised.

Our gospel reading teaches us that Christ is the new temple. He is God among us. While the prophet Ezekiel sees the temple in Jerusalem as the place of the presence of God, from which blessings flow out to renew and revive creation, Jesus is the new temple from whom new life comes in abundance.

But it is not a building of stones that we celebrate today. We celebrate the presence of Christ among us, his people, in his church. St Paul tells us that we ourselves are God's building, God's temple: 'Did you not realise that you were God's temple and that the Spirit of God was living among you?' The feast of this ancient basilica reminds us that we are 'living stones' and that we belong together in Christ's church.

Do I remember that I too am a temple of God, for the Holy Spirit has been given to me?

Do I value my membership of the Church, the new people of God in the world of today?

Let us thank God for the faith of those who have gone before us.

Let us pray for new Christians that they may grow in the faith.